The Scientific Revolution

A Captivating Guide to the Emergence of Modern Science During the Early Modern Period, Including Stories of Thinkers Such as Isaac Newton and René Descartes

© **Copyright 2019**

All Rights Reserved. No part of this book may be reproduced in any form without permission in writing from the author. Reviewers may quote brief passages in reviews.

Disclaimer: No part of this publication may be reproduced or transmitted in any form or by any means, mechanical or electronic, including photocopying or recording, or by any information storage and retrieval system, or transmitted by email without permission in writing from the publisher.

While all attempts have been made to verify the information provided in this publication, neither the author nor the publisher assumes any responsibility for errors, omissions or contrary interpretations of the subject matter herein.

This book is for entertainment purposes only. The views expressed are those of the author alone, and should not be taken as expert instruction or commands. The reader is responsible for his or her own actions.

Adherence to all applicable laws and regulations, including international, federal, state and local laws governing professional licensing, business practices, advertising and all other aspects of doing business in the US, Canada, UK or any other jurisdiction is the sole responsibility of the purchaser or reader.

Neither the author nor the publisher assumes any responsibility or liability whatsoever on the behalf of the purchaser or reader of these materials. Any perceived slight of any individual or organization is purely unintentional.

Free Bonus from Captivating History (Available for a Limited time)

Hi History Lovers!

Now you have a chance to join our exclusive history list so you can get your first history ebook for free as well as discounts and a potential to get more history books for free! Simply visit the link below to join.

Captivatinghistory.com/ebook

Also, make sure to follow us on Facebook, Twitter and Youtube by searching for Captivating History.

Contents

INTRODUCTION 1

CHAPTER 1 – SCIENCE: A DEFINITION AND BRIEF PREHISTORY 3

CHAPTER 2 – THE EARLY WESTERN SCIENCES 6

CHAPTER 3 - PARACELSUS 13

CHAPTER 4 – NICOLAUS COPERNICUS 18

CHAPTER 5 – LUIGI ANGUILLARA 23

CHAPTER 6 – ANDREAS VESALIUS 26

CHAPTER 7 – IGNAZIO DANTI 30

CHAPTER 8 – TYCHO AND SOPHIA BRAHE 34

CHAPTER 9 – PAUL WITTICH 39

CHAPTER 11 – JOSEPH GOEDENHUYZE 44

CHAPTER 12 – GIORDANO BRUNO 47

CHAPTER 13 – CONRAD GESSNER 52

CHAPTER 14 – JOHANNES KEPLER 56

CHAPTER 15 – DANIEL SENNERT 63

CHAPTER 16 – GALILEO GALILEI 67

CHAPTER 17 – WILLIAM HARVEY 72

CHAPTER 18 – RENÉ DESCARTES 76
CHAPTER 20 – ROBERT BOYLE 82
CHAPTER 21 – ANTONIE VAN LEEUWENHOEK 86
CHAPTER 22 – ISAAC NEWTON 90
CHAPTER 23 – ROBERT HOOKE 94
CHAPTER 24 – MARIA SIBYLLA MERIAN 98
CHAPTER 25 – MARIA WINCKELMANN-KIRCH 101
CHAPTER 26 – WILLIAM AND CAROLINE HERSCHEL 105
CHAPTER 27 – MARY SOMERVILLE 109
EPILOGUE 113

Introduction

Ancient cultures have been looking up at the stars for thousands of years, wondering about their place in the universe. What were those glowing spots in the black cover of night? Just how far away was the moon? These and other questions hounded humanity through the millennia until, finally, relative economic stability allowed for a number of people to examine their world more closely. Slowly, knowledge and understanding accumulated generation by generation until the conditions were ideal enough for a revolution to occur in thinking, experimentation, worldview, and natural philosophy.

It was the Scientific Revolution, the time period when Western theologians had more and better tools to measure and make sense of the things around them. With careful measurements, precise data collection, and an unwavering sense of curiosity, humankind stepped into the future. The truly magnificent feature of this time period, besides, of course, the scientific discoveries themselves, was the kinship between philosophers, scientists, and experimental hobbyists throughout Europe. Hundreds, if not thousands, of letters between great intellectuals such as Isaac Newton, Johannes Kepler, Robert Hooke, and Tycho Brahe have been preserved, demonstrating how these men (and a few women) worked in cooperation with one another in order to better their own research.

This was never so apparent as when the Royal Society of London was founded in 1660, functioning as a social club in which Europe's most learned minds could meet and discuss ideas. It was a most inspiring time when those with exciting theories about the state of the world and the universe came together to expand their research, publish and present their work, and receive the highest acclaim for doing so.

Of course, as in all periods of history, the Scientific Revolution was not without its poor, overlooked, or isolated figures. Amongst the applause and reverence, there was plenty of ostracization, criticism, sexism, and even martyrdom. Though the world was slowly becoming more tolerant, it was still a very dangerous time for some scientists and philosophers whose observations and ideas seemed to challenge the authority of the all-powerful Catholic Church. At the same time, religious beliefs played a large role in the evolving philosophies of science. Most chemists, physicists, and philosophers imagined God as something of a divine architect, whose most precious language was that of mathematics.

The countless men and women who conducted observations and experiments and painstakingly took notes during this crucial part of history successfully paved the way toward a more enlightened existence—one in which scientific method is the norm, rather than the exception.

Chapter 1 – Science: A Definition and Brief Prehistory

"The history of the sciences is a great fugue, in which the voices of the nations come one by one into notice."[1]

Science, as we know it today, is largely a product of the modern age, but forms of it have existed for thousands of years. "Scientia" is the Latin term from which our modern word was made, although it has undergone a metamorphosis.

The *Merriam-Webster Dictionary* defines "science" as:

"A department of systematized knowledge as an object of study…something (such as a sport or technique) that may be studied or learned like systematized knowledge."

Science, therefore, can be applied to virtually anything that can be observed and studied. Human behavior, fur patterns and colors in animals, plant growth, cellular structures, and many more topics can be studied in a scientific way, and since most of science's first subjects are derived directly from the natural world, the practice of their study was often called "natural philosophy" from the 5th century BCE in Greece up to the 19th century in Western Europe.

---

[1] Von Goethe, Johann Wolfgang, as quoted by James Wood. *Dictionary of Quotations from Ancient and Modern, English and Foreign Sources.* 1893.

Any practice in which a person gathers or uses data to draw conclusions about the nature of the universe (or a tiny piece of it) is science. That includes everything from solving mathematical equations to analyzing market data to determine the best way to sell a new product. In historical terms, the first formal sciences included mathematics, astronomy, and horticulture.

In prehistoric terms, farming techniques were one of the most important sciences ever undertaken. The earliest forms of science may appear as simple as observation of the things that humans needed for survival. The observation of animal migration patterns for hunting and the observation of the growing patterns of the foods people gathered could be considered their science. Humans had been mostly nomadic for tens of thousands of years—likely more—and they survived on a diet of fruits, vegetables, grains, and animals for which they hunted and scavenged. About 12,000 years ago in the Fertile Crescent of modern Iran, large groups of people started using agriculture to meet their nutritional needs instead of hunting and gathering.

At first, they probably used the seeds from the wild plants they ate to plant large swathes of edible foods, which they would visit frequently, and began to domesticate those plants. In time, however, as fields grew larger, people began to settle onto a patch of land that they worked for sustenance. Historians tell us that the first plants to be domesticated for food were two kinds of wheat, barley, flax, peas, lentils, chickpeas, and a type of vetch. Wild animals that were hunted for food would have been herded and kept contained as the very beginning of the domestication of animals for food by humans. It is theorized that smaller animals, such as goats and sheep, were the first to be contained and kept by these early farmers, and as people observed and developed better methods and tools, they began to domesticate larger animals. As they developed, they even incorporated these animals as tools themselves—oxen and other beasts of burden became the brute force needed for cultivating more land in a more consistent manner.

In sparking the Agricultural Revolution, also known as the Neolithic Revolution, those early peoples were conducting multitudes of scientific experiments. They were collecting seeds, and perhaps saplings and tubers, and figuring out which could be transplanted or sown into what sort of environment. It was a large-scale data collection that was analyzed according to which plants grew most readily and which of those produced a reasonable amount of food. They may have planted similar types of grains next to each other and watched to see which would work best for their crops. They may have planted them in different places and observed how some areas grew better crops. They would have observed that planting at different times produced different results. These first farmers would have observed how scattering seeds produced different results than scattering seeds and covering them with a bit of soil. All these observations and the collection of information about the different results from different methods was the science of this time.

Other prehistoric sciences include toolmaking and time-keeping according to the sun, moon, and stars. As people began to spend their time working on growing food and maintaining animals rather than trekking across vast areas to gather food and hunt animals, they would think of ways to make their new work easier. They would need different tools than what they had been using for their hunting and their gathering in the past. Toolmaking would be another chance for the early farmers to observe and test materials and ways of putting them together to make the things they needed for their new agricultural lifestyle.

All these developments from agriculture and the change from nomads to farmers came from the science of the time, which observed and collected information in order to improve on the new agrarian practices. These ancient scientific works were all about the necessity of humans to be able to eat and sustain their societies.

One might go so far as to say that science, in all its forms, has been a natural and inextricable part of the human experience.

Chapter 2 – The Early Western Sciences

"I am the wisest man alive, for I know one thing, and that is that I know nothing."[2]

Western civilization, which was centered first in Athens, then Rome, then perhaps Paris and London, first formally addressed a variety of sciences during classical antiquity. Proto-scientists of this era were generally called "philosophers," a word that meant "knowledge seeker." Starting in about the 5th century BCE and ending by the 3rd century CE, the period of classical antiquity was fundamental in setting out the first major tenets of scientific thought.

To the Greeks and Romans of that era, philosophy was perhaps the most important of the emerging sciences. Great thinkers like Plato and Socrates probed the inner workings of the human mind in search of patterns that could help predict future behaviors and emotional responses. Philosophy, though perhaps more related to the arts than modern science, nevertheless provided the first pieces of a puzzle that would eventually become psychology and psychiatry.

---

[2] Plato. *The Republic.*

The early Greek philosopher Plato was responsible for setting his nation on the path to its obsession with philosophy. He was very focused on understanding the role of mankind in the universe and yet was highly aware of the difficulties of coming up with answers to life's largest questions. Plato likened humankind's existence to that of a dark cave in which we can only face the far wall. Though there is a fire burning brightly behind us, illuminating truth and reality, all we can see are confusing shadows. Plato's extensive writings—usually in the form of dialogues in which the main character was his own revered tutor, Socrates—served not only as a sort of textbook for students of his own time but for students in the Renaissance and even the modern philosophy classroom.

Mathematics was also growing in leaps and bounds during this time period, and their usage in a variety of methods helped lay down the groundwork for strict data collection and analyzation in astronomy, economics, biology, and every single advanced scientific field. Pythagoras, a Greek philosopher whose personal beliefs led him to eat a plant-based diet and abhor violence, provided Greece, Rome, and their successors with multiple mathematical theories. He was first educated in Greece and then traveled to Egypt where he studied with monks in Memphis. There, he was captured as a prisoner of war and taken hostage to Syria, which is potentially where he figured out his most famous calculation: the Pythagorean Theorem.

Whether Pythagoras conceived of the theorem himself or adapted it from known mathematics in Syria and Egypt is unclear, but the fact that he returned to Greece with the knowledge is historically significant. It was a breakthrough into the field of trigonometry that instantly changed the way stargazers measured their findings in the sky. If they could line up their points of interest into a virtual equilateral triangle and determine the lengths of two sides, then the unknown length of the third side could be calculable.

Around the time Pythagoras was developing and teaching mathematics—notably to both females and males, in a time of strict sexism—he and other philosophers of the day were searching wildly for a unifying link between the various philosophies. Classical education for the wealthy and aristocrats of the Greco-Roman world consisted of lessons in reading, writing, arithmetic and other mathematics, music, oratory, and philosophy. Each subject was generally given equal importance with the others; therefore, every educated person knew something of mathematics, writing, and playing music, among other things. The logical question, for many philosophers, was how did all those facets of life fit together? After a time, they came to agree that the answer was math.

Math could be written about and explained, it could be used to describe musical notes and compositions, it helped map the stars and planets, and it could even be used to phrase universal questions, such as the weight of the world or the distance between the Earth and the Sun. Math even untangled the mystery of whether the Earth was closer to the Sun or the Moon.

In an effort to perfectly link all his fields of knowledge, Pythagoras posited that the Sun, Moon, stars, and all the planets emitted a specific musical tone. Though he could not hear it, the philosopher imagined that the solar system was full of beautiful music all in perfect scientific harmony. His philosophies and theories were so compelling that for hundreds of years after his death in about 495 BCE in Italy, the Pythagorean cult persisted in mathematical and philosophical pursuits while simultaneously avoiding meat in their diets. Vegetarianism was still referred to as the Pythagorean diet as late as the 19th century.

Of course, for the Greeks and Romans of classical antiquity, philosophy was the most popular and esteemed scientific pastime. Though warfare was at the heart of their culture, and strength and military prowess was long considered the worthiest of characteristics, an elite culture of intellectuals emerged who valued education and knowledge over brute strength. Few could afford such an outlook since the bulk of aristocrats and commoners spent their lives in military employ; however, the mindset, once fully grasped, would remain in the fabric of Western civilization.

When the Roman Empire annexed the former world power that was Greece, their society still respected Greek philosophers even over its own.[3] Roman rulers either sent their sons to Greece to be educated, or they bought a learned Greek slave to teach in their household. It was a custom that persisted for centuries, and it helped to keep the later Greco-Roman world largely homogenous. Both believed in an almost identical pantheon and obviously supported a similar type of educational curriculum, and though both truly valued democracy, it was undermined by the ambitions of their wealthy leaders.

The military might of both Greece and Rome meant that huge portions of Europe, Africa, the Middle East, and Asia were exposed to Greco-Roman-style administration and culture. In an effort to paint the world in their own likeness, conquerors like Alexander the Great and Julius Caesar quickly reinforced their newly won territories by giving local aristocrats and military leaders top roles in the new administration and also educating the next generation in the Greco-Roman style. Soon, the upper classes of these territories believed in the greatness of their conquerors just as much as the conquerors themselves did.

Therefore, by way of constant empire-expanding warfare and the extreme valuation of intellect and education, Greece and Rome imprinted both of those primary characteristics onto the whole of the Western world. It was thanks to the second that the pursuit of philosophy, then natural philosophy, and finally modern science and medicine were considered so important. Even as Europe rushed headlong into the future, caught up in religious wars, the boom and bust of kingdoms, and the constant need for more food and basic materials, those who had time to learn and reflect kept building on the scientific frameworks of their ancestors.

The Western Roman Empire collapsed during the 5th century CE, and when it shrank back to its foundations in Rome and failed even for a time to protect its legendary capital city, territories that had

---

[3] Crawford, Michael Hewson. *The Roman Republic.* 1993.

long been under the thumb of Roman imperialism were left to their own devices. Some of those lands were conquered by different external powers, and others rearranged themselves from within to create a new localized rule. This era has been classified by many modern historians as the Dark Ages—essentially, a period in Western history during which the metaphoric light of the Roman Empire ceased to shine. Local histories tell a slightly less exaggerated tale of the end of Roman rule, but in both cases, it was usually true that higher education took a backseat to the more pressing issues of food distribution, political administration, and infrastructure.

In many ways, the European continent of the Renaissance had changed from the continent that had largely been under the control of the Roman Empire. There were many formalized nation-states whose zig-zagging borders completed a patchwork of languages, cultures, and alliances, but their new common thread was Christianity. The Roman Empire had long since split into the Holy Roman Empire in the west and the Byzantine Empire in the east. The western realm was very politically fragmented, but the wealth and influence of the Church were sufficient enough to bind the collection of cities, duchies, and Italian states together under the same banner.

Renaissance Europe spanned the 14th to 17th centuries, beginning mostly in Florence and Venice and slowly stretching out to the west and north. Much of the information that flowed from region to region was in the form of scrolls and books, originally painstakingly copied letter by letter by monastery scribes. Books spread information, theories, and news, as well as a love of reading and writing. Johannes Gutenberg's printing press, developed in the mid-1400s, made book publishing immensely quicker, resulting in a great spike in book creation and sales.[4]

Though the poor and oppressed classes saw little change in their lives, save differences in agriculture and taxation, wealthier and

---

[4] Rees, Fran. *Johannes Gutenberg.* 2006.

more privileged people desired a return to the educational standards of classical antiquity. They revered knowledge and wanted to cultivate more of it, and in an effort to better mimic their learned Greek and Roman forebearers, authors and scientists throughout Europe studied and presented research in Latin.

From Italy to Germany to Britain, scholars published works of great importance first in Latin and then, perhaps a few years later, in their own vernacular. This fascination with Latin and all things classical made early modern students and professionals in every part of Europe able to communicate with their peers and colleagues elsewhere more easily, but it completely excluded the undereducated. Even with a very rudimentary knowledge of one's vernacular in terms of reading and writing, one couldn't make the leap from English, German, or Spanish, for example, to full Latin. It was as if the most important theories and developments of the age were coded and hidden before the eyes of the poor.

During the ensuing Scientific Revolution, higher education remained largely in the hands of sons of wealthy and aristocratic families of Europe. Because of this, science became the realm of upper-class white men, with just a few exceptions. Though it would eventually welcome women and people from other cultures more openly, early Western science was the domain of privileged—though certainly brilliant—males. The few women and people of color whose scientific work was actually peer-reviewed and supported during this era generally had to work much harder to achieve any kind of recognition in the field.

Nevertheless, the story of how science took over Europe is a fascinating one. The Scientific Revolution—a title given to this era by the 20th-century philosopher Alexandre Koyré–is generally believed to have spanned the centuries between Copernicus' publication of *De revolutionibus orbium coelestium* in 1543 and Isaac Newton's publication of *Philosophiæ Naturalis Principia*

Mathematica in 1687.[5] There was at least one exceptional member of the scientific community whose work should be mentioned before that of Copernicus, however, the doctor known as Paracelsus. Indeed, many more important discoveries were made during the 18th and 19th centuries that historians other than Koyré have deigned to include in their own interpretations of the Scientific Revolution.

This retelling begins with Paracelsus and comes to a close with the works of Mary Somerville, though it respectfully agrees that the heart of the era is fixed within the 16th and 17th centuries.

---

[5] Lindberg, David C. and Robert S. Westman. *Reappraisals of the Scientific Revolution*. 1993.

Chapter 3 - Paracelsus

1493/4–September 24, 1541

"He who knows nothing, loves nothing. He who can do nothing understands nothing. He who understands nothing is worthless. But he who understands also loves, notices, sees...The more knowledge is inherent in a thing, the greater the love...Anyone who imagines that all fruits ripen at the same time as the strawberries knows nothing about grapes."[6]

While Martin Luther railed against the Catholic Church and Copernicus anxiously scribbled notes for a book both Catholics and Martin Luther would come to abhor, a man named Theophrastus von Hohenheim pursued similar enlightenment in the deeply traditional lecture rooms of the continent's medical universities. Like his peers, von Hohenheim cultivated both faithful supporters and harshly critical detractors. The latter did not stop him from a wholehearted attempt to modernize and improve the field of medicine, however, and for his troubles, he earned the moniker of "father of toxicology."[7] He published many books under the name

---

[6] Paracelsus. *Paragranum.* 1530.
[7] Borzelleca, Joseph F. "Paracelsus: Herald of Modern Toxicology." *Oxford Academic Toxicological Sciences.* January 2000.

"Paracelsus," and this is how much of history remembers him. Though not all historians agree on the origins of this moniker, "Para Celsus" may have been Theophrastus' chosen name because it meant "equal to or greater than Celsus," Celsus having been a famed Roman physician in the 1st century.[8]

Born in Egg, a small village in modern Switzerland, von Hohenheim's father was a chemist whose scientific prowess surely influenced young Paracelsus. Some years later, the first place in which Paracelsus found employment was in the Venetian military, as a surgeon. After his service there, he set up his own medical practice in Basel, Switzerland, where he met the Dutch philosopher Erasmus of Rotterdam. The two struck up a friendship based on medicine and philosophy, and they began a long discourse on those subjects through letters.

Discourse and open communication were very important to Paracelsus, who lectured at the University of Basel in the language of German rather than Latin. He did not want to limit his students, and he knew that German was more widely understood by people of all classes. It was a point of contention with him that his lectures be available—and comprehensible—to everyone who wished to attend. Other lecturers and university members disagreed, but this was only one of many of Paracelsus' nonconformist and controversial notions. He also harshly criticized his fellow medical lecturers and colleagues at the university, and he publicly burned the traditional teaching texts of the ancient Greek physician Galen and the 11th-century Persian doctor, Avicenna.

Most physicians of the 16th century were more interested in balancing the humors. According to the ancient Greeks, there were four humors, or vital facets, to one's life force: black bile, yellow bile, blood, and phlegm. Each of these represented different qualities. Black bile was dry and cold, while yellow bile was dry and

---

[8] Hargrave, John G. "Paracelsus, German-Swiss Physician."

hot; blood was wet and hot, while phlegm was wet and cold. Ancient physicians believed that illness was caused by one or more of these humors either over- or under-functioning; therefore, bringing them back into balance would cure any ailment.

The four humors were so integral to medicine and one's lifestyle that they were equated to many other parts of nature, such as the four seasons and the supposed four different temperaments. Practitioners referred to black bile, yellow bile, blood, and phlegm as the melancholic, choleric, sanguine, and phlegmatic humors, which referred to moodiness, bad-temperedness, courageousness, and calm, unemotional temperaments, respectively. In humor-balancing medicine, physicians were responsible for tempering whichever humor they perceived to be out of balance. For example, if a person was described as frantic or manic, they would be diagnosed with having too much blood; the cure, therefore, was a simple bleeding procedure.

While most medicine still focused on the treatment of one's humors, Paracelsus decided to look beyond the superficial symptoms of sickness. He was interested in what might be happening on a chemical level when a patient began to exhibit signs of disease. He found it necessary to test all scientific theories, and he also told his students that it was necessary to travel extensively in search of tried-and-true procedures. He explained that the truths of medicine lay not only in the hands of doctors but with old women, housewives, gypsies, and wandering tribes. Paracelsus knew that the information he needed was everywhere, if only he could find it and test it.

Paracelsus himself spent years traveling throughout Europe, Asia, and North Africa, collecting data and learning about the different methods used by physicians and scientists in other parts of the world. Paracelsus was fascinated with Arabian chemistry in particular, and it is rumored that he was given the secret of a universal solvent by an Arab chemist. More importantly to the development of Western medicine, perhaps, was Paracelsus' attention to the scientific method. It served him extremely well during his time as a military surgeon with the Hapsburg armies, who were under the authority of King Charles I of Spain, Holy Roman Emperor. King Charles I was almost constantly at war against France and the Ottoman Empire, which meant that his armies had little time to rest and recuperate.

Paracelsus attended the wounded as best he could, at first using the widely accepted method of treating open wounds with boiling oil. It was yet another method derived from the belief in treating the humors; since war wounds from weapons were generally bloody and hot, they were tended with heat in an attempt to replenish the body's lost heat. Even university-trained doctors believed in this dogma, and Paracelsus had little reason to doubt this time-honored method until one day he ran out of oil. In its place, he desperately collected soothing herbs and ointments to use instead. The next day, an unprecedented number of the wounded soldiers had survived. It was clear to Paracelsus that the different treatment must have impacted the survival rate; he persevered without hot oil and realized that wound treatment with cleansing and soothing materials had a much better outcome.

Paracelsus wrote of his discovery in his 1536 book *Die große Wundarzney*, whose title roughly translates to English as "Great Book of Surgery." His was not the only treatise on the development of medicinal treatments without hot oil and other aggressive, unclean forms of salve; French physician Ambroise Paré came to a similar conclusion during his own experiences with patients. Regardless of who did indeed first remove hot oil (and cattle dung) from his medical kit, it was an astoundingly important step forward in science and medicine.

Wound treatment was not the only advancement made by Paracelsus. He also studied the rampant illness known as syphilis in hopes that he might learn how to alleviate or prevent the symptoms of sores, rashes, vision loss, hearing loss, pain, and dementia. Since the disease had recently been imported from the West Indies, medieval physicians believed they could rid people of the disease by smothering them in wood, smoke, and pastes created from trees also taken from the New World. This method was quite ineffective, however, and Paracelsus believed he could find a better one.

Since Paracelsus and other scientists thought that syphilis was related to leprosy, and since Arab physicians had some success treating the latter with mercury, he thought it would be worth trying with victims of syphilis. The treatments could have caused mouth ulcers and loose teeth, and a truly effective treatment would not be discovered until 1910. Since the second phase of syphilis infection was a non-symptomatic phase that lasted for years, it is difficult to judge whether the mercurial treatment was useful or not.

Regardless of his mistakes, Paracelsus' insistence on exploring every possible theory and his potential revelation on wound cleansing were extremely influential on the later characters of the Scientific Revolution.

Chapter 4 – Nicolaus Copernicus

February 19, 1473–May 24, 1543

"To know the mighty works of God, to comprehend His wisdom and majesty and power; to appreciate, in degree, the wonderful workings of His laws, surely all this must be a pleasing and acceptable mode of worship to the Most High, to whom ignorance cannot be more grateful than knowledge."[9]

For astronomers and astrologists of the Renaissance, there was one major, ongoing argument: Was the Earth the center of the universe, or was it the Sun? Heliocentrism versus geocentrism had been an ongoing debate since astronomers began mapping the stars and planets of the universe, but in the Renaissance, the division between the two became especially pronounced. The issue put a great deal of pressure on scientists and clergymen since it potentially undermined the teachings of the Christian Bible.

According to the Catholic Church, which wielded the vast majority of political and financial power at the time in Europe, there were two reasons why scientific announcements about the structure of the universe were generally treated with derision. The first reason had to do with the Church's sense of divine authority; members of the

---

[9] Van Norman, Louis E. *Poland: The Knight Among Nations.* 1907.

clergy had inherited a religious organization in which they and their predecessors were considered the primary source of knowledge and wisdom for the people. Scientists who studied at universities not directly under the authority of the Church, therefore, were often seen as rivals to the Church, although there were many religious scientists whose findings and persecutions forced them to abandon their roles as members of the clergy.

The second reason for pushback against the idea of a heliocentric universe was that most members of the high clergy found a geocentric universe more comforting than other scientific models. It seemed to fit the outlines of the Bible more precisely, so, therefore, Christian scientists—of whom there was a great deal—began their astronomical studies under the fundamental assumption that the Earth was the center of all creation.

Nicolaus Copernicus, a Prussian astronomer, although some place his nationality as being Polish, didn't think the evidence added up in favor of a geocentric universe, however. He had been educated at the University of Bologna and the University of Kraków, and he also had the benefit of sharing a residency with none other than the university's main astronomer: Domenico Maria de Novara. During his time in Bologna, Copernicus assisted de Novara with the important work of casting astrological charts for the nobility, members of the clergy, and other social groups of the city. At the time, astronomy and astrology were not only inextricably linked, but they were both highly respected endeavors. Through his studies and work alongside de Novara, Copernicus learned the basic calculations and astronomical observations necessary to take up a career in either science.

On March 9, 1497, the pair witnessed the moon eclipse the star Alpha Tauri. It was an event that Copernicus took special note of, although at the time, he was probably constructing astrological charts and not innovative new theories in the field. Later, however, that eclipse helped him work out the diameter of the moon to within a few degrees.

After leaving Bologna, Copernicus moved on to study medicine, and in 1503, he actually received a doctorate in canon law from the University of Ferrara.[10] A true polymath of his day, Copernicus had a diverse and marvelously well-rounded education, as was the fashion for well-financed boys of the time. His career upon graduation was within the Catholic Church.

A decade after earning his doctorate, Copernicus found himself managing the day-to-day activities and business of renters and tradesmen within church lands in a parish of Frombork, Poland. He also worked as a teacher, but he pursued astronomy in the little spare time left to him. Copernicus' work over the course of his life allowed him to collect a significant amount of data, which he arranged in a book called *De revolutionibus orbium coelestium* (or in English, *On the Revolutions of the Heavenly Spheres*). Full of innovative scientific breakthroughs, *De revolutionibus* contained three revolutionary propositions:

1: All the known planets, including Earth, travel in a fixed orbit around the Sun.

2: Earth spins once daily on its axis. This movement creates night and day, as the part of Earth we live on first faces the Sun and then turns away from it. The angle of the Earth's axis, which is 23.5 degrees, gives our planet seasons. During the part of Earth's orbit when its axis leans toward the Sun, we have summer. When the axis leans away, we have winter. The Northern and Southern Hemispheres experience seasons differently since when the Northern Hemisphere leans toward the Sun, the Southern Hemisphere leans away. Therefore, when it is summer in Europe, it is winter in Australia.

3: The Earth's axis precesses, or rotates, slowly in the opposite direction to the axial spin, a movement that is responsible for the

---

[10] Gingerich, Owen and James MacLachlan. *Nicholas Copernicus: Making the Earth a Planet.* 2005.

changing orientation of the North and South Poles. Though the North Star is currently Polaris, this will slowly change over the course of our planet's 26,000-year precession cycle.

Copernicus wrote: "The apparent...motion of the planets arises not from their motion but from the Earth's. The motion of the Earth alone, therefore, suffices to explain so many apparent inequalities in the heavens."[11]

To Copernicus, these discoveries were both satisfying and elegant—every philosopher's dream since Plato and Aristotle had gazed at the stars and attempted to explain their movement centuries ago in Greece. The notions of precession, axial rotation, and heliocentrism were not unique to Copernicus, but his confidence in their truth was a very important step forward in European astronomy. Of course, the most controversial theory was that of the Sun sitting at the center of everything instead of the Earth. Copernicus insisted:

> In the middle of all sits Sun enthroned. In this most beautiful temple could we place this luminary in any better position from which he can illuminate the whole at once?...So the Sun sits as upon a royal throne ruling his children the planets which circle round him The Earth has the Moon at her service.[12]

Fully aware that he would need to defend his theories both from his scientific peers and members of the clergy, Copernicus spent decades fine-tuning his book to make sure it was as flawless as possible. In fact, that book, *De revolutionibus,* didn't make it to the printing press until 1543, just two months before the astronomer died. Copernicus included a letter to Pope Paul III, entreating him to accept this fully formed theory of a heliocentric universe.

Copernicus lay dying as his book was finally copied and bound, and it's unlikely he ever saw a finished copy of the manuscript which so

---

[11] "Exploring the Planets, The Renaissance, Copernicus." *Smithsonian National Air and Space Museum.* Web.
[12] Copernicus, Nicolas. *De revolutionibus.* 1543.

many future scientists would ruminate on so seriously. Perhaps purposefully, the author of *De revolutionibus* had made his book very technical in nature so that the general population would have struggled to make sense of it. Because of this, the book sold very few copies and only went into the hands of educated astronomers who could understand the illustrations and calculations done by Copernicus. With little public criticism, *De revolutionibus* quietly revolutionized Europe's astronomical societies, from England to Italy.

Chapter 5 – Luigi Anguillara

c. 1512–September 1570

"[Luigi Anguillara's botanical garden at Padua] is the origin of all the botanical gardens in the world, a cradle of science and scientific exchange, serving as the basis for the understanding of the relationship between nature and culture. It largely contributed to the progress of a number of modern scientific fields, the likes of which include, of course, botanicals, as well as medicine, chemistry, ecology and pharmaceuticals."[13]

The Age of Discovery had started at the beginning of the 15th century, and while it did start before the Scientific Revolution, it coincided with it for the most part, making it an important factor in the development of the Revolution. When Christopher Columbus discovered new islands far to the west of Europe in 1492, his voyages were immediately followed by explorers and conquerors from various European nations, including France, England, the Netherlands, and Portugal. Soon, both North and South America were crawling with Europeans in search of gold and anything else valuable to sell back home. They brought precious metals, indigenous peoples, and boatloads of plant foods.

Conventional European botany—and food preparation—were forever and unalterably changed due to this change. Suddenly, the Old World was full of corn, potatoes, tomatoes, bell peppers, chili peppers, tobacco, and much more. All of it needed to be categorized, tested, retested, and documented. Noted botanist and herb collector Luigi Anguillara stepped up to the challenge, excited to discover the potential uses for each new species of plant. He spent decades exploring the Mediterranean and observing the flora he found at each new port, as well as those exotic samples from across the Atlantic Ocean.

In 1539, Anguillara began spending a lot of time at the private botanical garden of Luca Ghini in Bologna.[14] The two worked together in pursuit of horticultural knowledge as well as the cultivation of various species of plants to be used for scientific study and observation. The garden was moved to Pisa in 1544, and Anguillara remained a frequent visitor until he was made the first director of Orto Botanico di Padova, the botanical gardens in Padua.[15] The Padua botanical gardens, already the oldest in Europe, would become his legacy.[16] It grew under his supervision and gained a reputation with scientific students and authors all throughout Europe, who visited the gardens for educational purposes. When, in 1561, Anguillara was offered the position of personal herbalist to the Duke of Ferrara, he accepted the position and moved on in search of yet more species to document.[17] The gardens at Padua remained a public spectacle in his absence, but the botanist's reputation remained with them.

---

[13] Pamphlet of the Botanical Garden of Padua, as quoted in "Discovering the Botanical Garden of Padua." *Go UNESCO!* 2016.
[14] "Anguillara, Luigi - - [The Greatest Book of Botany Ever Written in Italy] ." *ViaLibri.* Web.
[15] Ibid.
[16] There is debate over the oldest botanical garden in Europe, between Padua and Pisa—proponents of Padua's claim say that since Pisa's garden was moved, it dropped to becoming the second oldest.

[17] Ibid.

In 1561, Anguillara published *Semplici,* a descriptive catalog of 1,540 plant species that included their inherent medicinal qualities as well as their natural geographical locations. It was a very timely document, not only because of the emergence of botany and other scientific pursuits, but because of the fact that Europe's explorers had just recently discovered a plethora of new plant species on the other side of the Atlantic Ocean. The book's name translates to "Simplism," the contemporary word for collecting medicinal herbs, and its author is considered one of the greatest Simplists of his era.

Chapter 6 – Andreas Vesalius

December 31, 1514–October 15, 1564

"Aristotle and many others say men have more teeth than women; it is no harder for anyone to test this than it is for me to say it is false, since no one is prevented from counting teeth."[18]

Botany and horticulture such as that undertaken by Anguillara and his peers remained inextricably bound with medicine and the application of treatments. Physicians of the Middle Ages and the early modern era concocted their remedies with primarily plants, though sometimes minerals and other materials were included in their recipes. Verbena and sage were applied to the bodies of patients suffering from high fevers, although blood-letting was also a popular treatment for such a state.

A forward-thinking physician from Brussels, by the name of Andreas Vesalius, shared a professional link with Luigi Anguillara at Padua, Italy. Vesalius first inhabited the city while studying for his medical degree at the University of Padua, and after graduation, he stayed on as a lecturer in the 1530s and into the 1540s.[19] His tenure

---

[18] Vesalius, Andreas. *De humani corporis fabrica libri septem.* 1543.
[19] Florken, Marcel. "Andreas Vesalius, Belgian physician." *Encyclopedia Britannica.* Web. 28 May 2019.

at the university likely coincided with that of Luigi Anguillara at the botanical gardens. Whether the two scientists met face to face or not, they probably knew of one another and had some level of insight into the other's methodology as it related to natural philosophy. While Anguillara painstakingly observed, dissected, and cataloged vast collections of plant species, Vesalius could not have helped feeling a frustrated jealousy toward his scientific peer for the former's freedom in his studies. In fact, Anguillara's hands-on approach may have helped inspire Vesalius to take the same tack in his own work: human anatomy.

Vesalius knew that medical advancements could only go so far without an in-depth knowledge of the human body, and he suspected that the anatomical reports published by the ancient Greek physician Galen were not firsthand but based on the dissection of animals. The Greeks and Romans, he knew, did not support human dissection, and only two notable ancient physicians had definitely undertaken such an endeavor: Herophilus of Chalcedon and Erasistratus of Ceos.[20]

Human dissection was not performed again in the ancient kingdoms—at least not officially and on record—since the 3rd century BCE. Vesalius and other Renaissance physicians and scientists were also not in the habit of such a practice, not least because it would have been socially unacceptable in most situations. Not even personal medical examinations by physicians were conducted in the absence of the patient's clothing, and, therefore, an intimate understanding of the human body was quite limited. Even scientists and physicians who examined the bodies of dead people were only able to do so sparingly, and it took centuries before anything resembling humanity's true anatomy was in the hands of European medical schools or even the continent's general practitioners. That era began largely in part to Andreas Vesalius,

---

[20] Von Staden, H. "The discovery of the body: human dissection and its cultural contexts in ancient Greece." *Yale Journal of Biology and Medicine.* May/June 1992.

whose urge to discover the true complexities of the human body for himself led him to obtain and dissect multiple cadavers.

Andreas Vesalius spent years dissecting corpses to learn how the parts of the inner body were positioned and how they might interact with one another. He performed these autopsies and exploratory dissections in the presence of students so that they might all benefit from the research. It wasn't the first time cadavers had been cut open in Renaissance Europe—in fact, in 14th-century Italy, Leonardo da Vinci pored over the bodies of corpses he was allowed to examine so that he could become a better artist. In fact, da Vinci's anatomical drawings are considered one of his most valuable contributions to the modern world.

Likewise, a few centuries after da Vinci's own drawings had been expertly completed, Vesalius probed even further into the body. His masterwork, *De humani corporis fabrica* (or in English, *On the Fabric of the Human Body*) was printed in 1543. Its pages were filled with elegant, highly detailed depictions of the skeletal system, muscle groups, the intestines and stomach, kidneys, liver, and even the entire venous system. Men and women were both included in the books, and many of the figures were drawn in apparent despair, posed in a frightened and furious stance, their head thrown up to the sky in agony. Still, others seemed quite at ease, even jaunty and jovial. He published another version of the same work around this time called *De humani corporis fabrica librorum epitome* (or in English, *Abridgement of the Structure of the Human Body*). This book placed more emphasis on the illustrations and, as the title suggests, was an abridged version of his original work. These books were an astounding accomplishment, both on a personal level and in the scientific realm.

Vesalius' cadaver studies revealed several differences between the true anatomical structure of humans and the structure long ago proposed by Galen. The Renaissance physician discovered that the collection of blood vessels just under the brain as depicted by Galen—found in some types of animals—was, in fact, not present in the human body. He also found that the human lower jaw was one bone, not two, and Galen's supposed holes between blood ventricles could not be located anywhere.

Other European physicians were shocked at Vesalius' assertion that Galen's work was flawed, and many scientists, holy people and members of the public, were outraged that he dared to cut open human bodies. When Vesalius left Spain, where he had taken a position originally as a physician to Emperor Charles V and then his son, King Philip II, it was rumored that his subsequent pilgrimage to Jerusalem in 1564 was undertaken to absolve him of his sins of cutting into human bodies. On the return journey, Vesalius' ship was wrecked on the Greek island of Zakynthos. The doctor climbed onto the rocky shore to save himself, but he soon fell ill and died there.

The multitude of anatomical drawings completed and published by Andreas Vesalius richly benefited the contemporary medical community, and although his work was abhorred by many, it was vastly appreciated by his students. At the urging of their teacher, Vesalius' medical students carried out their own human dissections and helped shift the view of such learning methods into a positive light, at least in scientific circles. Before the Scientific Revolution came to a close, thousands more dissections would take place.

Chapter 7 – Ignazio Danti

April 1536–October 19, 1586

"The Pope was desirous that the walls should also serve the cause of science, and ordered the compartments to be adorned with geographical delineations of ancient and modern Italy, a task designated to Padre Ignazio Danti, a Dominican, a mathematician and geographer of his court."[21]

Human dissection and illustrations of the human body continued to have an impact on the arts, just as they did on medicine. For painters and sculptors, such as those in the Danti family, knowledge of subcutaneous anatomy helped in the process of mapping out very detailed human figures. During the Renaissance, human figures often took on a much more realistic bent in European art, largely thanks to an understanding of the muscular and skeletal structures beneath the skin.

In 1536, a boy named Pellegrino was born into the Danti family in Perugia, Italy. During his childhood, he was taught the fundamentals of painting, sculpting, and architecture by his family members. Though his brothers would become professional artists, Pellegrino decided to enter the Dominican Order at the age of 18 in March

---

[21] Lanzi, A. L. *The history of painting in Italy Volume I.* 1847.

1555, which was when he changed his first name to Ignazio (sometimes spelled as Egnatio or Egnazio). With the Dominicans, Danti was schooled in philosophy, theology, Christianity, and the sciences. Though at first he pursued preaching, it was not long before Ignazio admitted having a keener interest in mathematics and astronomy.

The monk was transferred to the monastery in Florence in 1562 upon his own request, and once there, he became a part-time science tutor for the city's wealthy children. The move to Florence proved to be life-changing for Danti, not just because of his tutoring jobs but because the Duke of Florence, Cosimo I de' Medici, took note of his scientific prowess and asked him to join an exciting project. De' Medici was renovating the Palazzo Vecchio, Florence's town hall, and within the building, he was planning a special gallery of maps called the Guardaroba. His plan for the Guardaroba was to display finely detailed mural maps of the world surrounded by a variety of contemporary scientific instruments, such as clocks and telescopes. The purpose of the space was to display some of the collected items of the illustrious de' Medici family.

Danti's part in the project was to paint 57 decorative maps onto the doors of a large cabinet that stood along the walls of the Guardaroba. Each map corresponded to several objects in the de' Medici's collection. Danti undertook the work gladly, his natural interest in geography mingling with the artistic education he had received at a young age. He painted beautiful renditions of many regions of the four known continents of the Earth: Europe, Africa, Asia, and the Americas.

Danti was very interested in cartography, but he himself was not an explorer. To paint the cabinet murals in the Guardaroba of the Palazzo Vecchio, he relied on the works of his contemporaries in those fields, including Giacomo Gastaldi, Abraham Ortelius, and Gerardus Mercator. In addition to the murals, Danti also worked on a giant central feature of the Guardaroba: a globe of the Earth. His contributions to the Palazzo Vecchio satisfied his natural desire for a scientific occupation, especially because the renovations there took many years to complete. In fact, Cosimo de' Medici died in 1574 before his entire vision for the Palazzo Vecchio had been finished.[22] The project was grandiose even in its unfinished state, however, and Danti's involvement there led to more opportunities for him to stretch his artistic and scientific wings.

One of those opportunities came directly from Pope Gregory XIII. The office of the papacy was very familiar with the political leaders of Florence, since members of the de' Medici family were very high up in the Catholic Church, with several of them serving their turn as the pope. Though Gregory XIII was not a part of the de' Medici family, he was nevertheless aware of Danti's work with Cosimo before the latter's death. In need of a mathematician to assist his own science team with the production of the Vatican's calendar, Gregory XIII invited Danti to Rome.

Danti accepted the position of pontifical mathematician, as well as membership in the commission in charge of reforming the calendar. It was in the latter position that Danti made his most lasting contribution to the Scientific Revolution, as he helped to calculate the structure for Europe's new Gregorian calendar.

Up until that point, the continent followed the Julian calendar, which had been in use since its introduction in 45 BCE by the Roman dictator Julius Caesar.[23] Though the Julian calendar had corrected many inconsistencies in its predecessor, the Roman calendar, its function as a timekeeper was still imprecise by 11 minutes per year. For that reason, the months of the year which had originally occurred in winter or summer had rotated out of step with the seasons. Easter, a highly important and celebrated holiday in the Christian religions, was thereby displaced several months away from the Spring Equinox upon which it was traditionally observed. Pope Gregory XIII was unsatisfied with the shortfalls of the Julian calendar and was

---

[22] Middleton, John. *World Monarchies and Dynasties.* 2015.
[23] "The Julian Calendar." *TimeandDate.com.* Web.

determined to create a more precise version. To that end, he hired a team of mathematicians that included Ignazio Danti.

Danti and his colleagues were able to create an annual calendar of 12 months that only differed from the true solar year by 26 seconds. Though this will still slowly rotate out of time with the seasons, it will only be one day ahead of the solar year by 4909.[24] The first version of the Gregorian calendar was made public in October 1582. The next year, the pope made Ignazio Danti the Bishop of Alatri in the small town of Campagna in southern Italy. In addition to his mathematical work for the pope, Danti was also commissioned by Gregory XII to paint several large frescoes in the Gallery of Maps, located in the Vatican Palace. He spent three years painting forty large, detailed maps of the regions of Italy.

Danti traveled to Rome in 1586 at the request of Pope Sixtus V to assist the architect Domenico Fontana in removing the Egyptian obelisk from its place in the circus of the Vatican. The obelisk had been brought to Rome in the 1st century CE, and Danti and Fontana re-erected it where it now stands in the center of St. Peter's Square in the Vatican. After his return from this trip to Rome, Danti contracted pneumonia from which he died.[25]

---

[24] Cohen, Jenny. "6 Things You May Not Know About the Gregorian Calendar." *History.com*. Web. 29 May 2019.
[25] O'Connor, J. J. and E. F. Robertson. "Egnatio Pellegrino Rainaldi Danti." Web. *University of St. Andrews*. November 2002.

Chapter 8 – Tycho and Sophia Brahe

December 14, 1546–October 24, 1601 | August 24, 1559–1643

"So Mathematical Truth prefers simple words since the language of Truth is itself simple."[26]

Danish astronomer Tycho Brahe did not agree with the Copernican model of the universe. Instead, he endeavored to collect a vast amount of astronomical data to prove the universe was, in fact, geocentric and that the Sun revolved around the Earth.

Tycho came from a wealthy family who saw to it that he received an excellent education, but the young man's hotheadedness resulted in a serious facial disfigurement at the age of 20.[27] Having lost part of his nose in a sword fight with his own cousin—over an ongoing argument over who was the better mathematician—Brahe henceforth wore a brass prosthetic glued over the injury.[28]

---

[26] Brahe, Tycho. *Epistolarum astronomicarum liber primus*. 1596.
[27] Hamilton, David. *A History of Organ Transplantation*. 2012.
[28] Gannon, Megan. "Tycho Brahe Died from Pee, Not Poison." November 16 2012.

Geocentrism certainly paid better than heliocentrism; Brahe was patronized by King Frederick II of Denmark, not only to continue his astronomical studies but to design and build an entire research facility on the island of Hven. With Frederick's funding, Brahe built Uraniborg between 1576 and 1580, a research institute where he built modern instruments to act as a high-tech astronomical observatory. Brahe spared none of his patron's expense, either; in his 1598 book, *Astronomiae instauratae mechanica* (or in English, *Instruments for the Restoration of Astronomy*), he included careful, colorful illustrations of his immense facility. Surrounded by a huge, square rammed-earth wall lay the grounds of the facility, which were painstakingly landscaped and symmetrically tiled. At the center of the tile work lay the main building, which resembled a French castle, complete with multiple blue-capped turrets. It was nothing less than a palace of astronomy. Since Urania was the ancient Greek god of astronomy, Brahe named his facility Uraniborg.

Within the vast walls of Uraniborg, Brahe undertook myriad measurements and notes as he observed the movements of the heavens from the castle's high central observatory. Interestingly, though lens making had been underway in Europe for centuries (eyeglasses were probably first invented in Pisa in the 13th century),[29] the telescope was still a few decades from being invented (the earliest known telescope to exist was made in 1608). Therefore, Brahe's magnificent observatory was completely unable to provide magnification. Before the construction of Uraniborg was even completed, however, Brahe realized that his plan to mount delicate astronomical instruments to the towers of the castle was not feasible due to the high winds. So, he had his large mural quadrant mounted in the main building and looked for another option for his other tools.

Many of these instruments were moved into an underground laboratory that Tycho designed partway through the construction of

---

[29] Ilardi, Vincent. *Renaissance Vision from Spectacles to Telescopes*. 2007.

Uraniborg. He called this underground facility Stjerneborg. There, he and his team built and used instruments like the free-standing azimuth quadrant, a similar creation to the sundial but aimed at a range of astral bodies; a great globe depicting the Earth; an armillary sphere; and various versions of these initial tools. Since Stjerneborg allowed for stargazing instruments to peek out the top of the roof at ground level, Tycho could accurately take measurements and take better care of his delicate, finely wrought instruments.

In the main building, the mural quadrant was erected onto a north-south wall where it was used to measure the altitude of the sun, moon, and stars as they passed by. Tycho took painstaking notes and kept volumes of records concerning the movements of the astral bodies, and he developed an interesting theory to explain how those movements supported his geocentric view of the universe. He proposed that while all the other planets of the solar system did indeed seem to orbit around the Sun, Earth's Moon and the Sun itself actually orbited around the Earth.

The island of Hven became an economic microcosm in itself, with Tycho Brahe as the head of all departments, both formal and informal. He endeavored to act in the best interests of the staff employed at his palace of science, going so far as to construct manufacturing centers, a paper mill, and housing for everyone involved.

Though Tycho's immense lab was full of staff, he constantly felt the need to hire more assistants. Fortunately, he had a regular and willing assistant in his own sister, Sophia. About thirteen years younger than her famous brother, Sophia learned horticulture and chemistry from Tycho but taught herself astronomy by studying books she paid to have translated into German. She began assisting her brother with his astronomical work at the age of seventeen, and Tycho took great pride in her scientific aptitude.

At Uraniborg, Sophia helped her brother chart the stars, track the progress of planets, and create horoscopes. When she wasn't peering closely at quadrants at Uraniborg, Sophia was creating breathtaking gardens in Eriksholm, Denmark. Her skills in horticulture and landscaping were widely acclaimed, and her knowledge of chemistry and astronomy were well known in the contemporary scientific community. Her parents, however, were embarrassed and angry at their daughter's choice to pursue science. The family was very well-off but exceptionally traditional, and they expected Sophia to conform to the role of wife and mother.

Against her parents' wishes, Sophia continued to follow her natural interests. Beside Tycho and a long line of highly respected astronomers, philosophers, and other great minds of the day, Sophia helped her brother make his most important assertion: the stars were not fixed in the sky. Careful, painstaking observation and nearly endless stacks of notes, charts, and journals led Tycho to the confident declaration that the stars of the night sky were, in fact, on a constant journey, not unlike that of the Moon and planets.

In 1572, Tycho discovered what he called a "new star" among the lights of the constellation Cassiopeia on November 11.[30] He recorded his observations in fine detail and measured the anomaly on his star charts so precisely that it was agreed among his peers that the new star was not a nearby comet but something out in the distance of the fixed stars. It was the size of Venus and visible to the naked eye until March of 1574.[31]

A comet passed overhead from November 1577 to January 1578, and Tycho's precise observations and calculations allowed him to prove that the distance between the Earth and the comet was greater than the distance between the Earth and the Moon. This helped solidify his theory that the stars did not exist in a constant, fixed state since the comet clearly had come from somewhere outside the Earth's realm. Sophia aided as always in the calculations and

---

[30] "Tycho's Nova." *Encyclopedia Britannica*. Web.

[31] Ibid.

documentation of what would be, centuries later, classified as a supernova. In 1573, Tycho published *De nova et nullius aevi memoria prius visa stella,* which translates into English as "Concerning the Star, New and Never Before Seen in the Life or Memory of Anyone."

Tycho was not the only Brahe family member favored by the Danish king; although Sophia was cut off financially from her family's money, King Frederick II of Denmark put Sophia's name on the deed to a farm in Sweden in 1587.[32] She was able to support herself for a time, moving about Denmark and Sweden regularly to work on landscaping projects and astronomical observations at Uraniborg.

Despite having her own property, Sophia found herself living in extreme poverty for several years after the turn of the 17th century while arranging her wedding to Erik Lange. Lange, a man of science who was passionate about alchemy, apparently used up all of his and Sophia's money attempting to transmute base metals into gold. According to a letter that Sophia wrote to her sister Margaret at the time, she wore ripped stockings on her wedding day while Lange had to return his wedding suit to the pawnshop after the ceremony.[33] When Lange died, deeply in debt, in 1613, Sophia settled on the Danish island of Zealand where she spent her own final years working with plants and writing the genealogical histories of various Danish aristocratic families.

Tycho stayed at Uraniborg full-time until 1597, meeting with a series of intellectuals from all parts of Europe during his two decades there.

---

[32] Svensson, Rebecka; Bengtsson, Caroline; and Lisa Jönsson. "Årup."
[33] Ibid.

Chapter 9 – Paul Wittich

c. 1546–January 9, 1586

"Wittich had poor eyes and should have stuck to geometry. However, as a theoretician, Wittich soon displayed talents."[34]

In 1580, Paul Wittich arrived at Uraniborg and stayed for several months to assist with astronomical observations there.[35]

> Tycho held nothing back as he explained the novel star-sights and scales on his quadrants, sextants, and armillary spheres. They toured the library with its thousands of books and its giant celestial globe, and they swapped notes on their ingenious trigonometrical methods. And the quest [Wittich] showed his host [Tycho] the technical underpinnings of his cosmological speculations...The idea of preserving some of the Copernican details, but with the Earth as the fixed centre, must have greatly intrigued Tycho.[36]

---

[34] Thoren, Victor E. and John Robert Christianson. *The Lord of Uraniborg.* 1990.

[35] Dreyer, J. L. E. "On Tycho Brahe's Manual of Trigonometry." *The Observatory.* 1916.

[36] Gingerich, O. *The Book Nobody Read: Chasing the Revolutions of Nicolaus Copernicus.* 2004.

The free-flow of ideas between the two men was exhilarating, at least for Brahe, who wrote of the high regard he had for Wittich in letters to his colleagues. Ironically, though, Wittich is seldom remembered in the modern histories of that era, even though he was probably responsible for a great deal of the mathematical labor that went into Uraniborg's daily research.

Together, Brahe and Wittich worked on prosthaphaeresis, a mathematical precursor to the logarithm that helped astronomers and sailors measure the true location of astral bodies using their average locations in the sky. This involved an accurate measurement of parallax, which the two studied extensively. An object's parallax is its perceived difference in location as judged from two different lines of sight—a good example of parallax is the apparent shift of an object as viewed from one's right eye versus one's left eye. Parallax was already being used by astronomers to calculate the distance between two objects, thanks to the trigonometric discoveries of Pythagoras in ancient Greece; in fact, Pythagoras probably learned about this mathematical relationship during his time with the Egyptians or Syrians.

Wittich and Brahe carefully monitored and recorded the positions of the visible planets, using trigonometry to try to establish their distance from one another. They were also attempting to discern the correct order in which they orbited the Earth (it had yet to be accepted that the planets in our solar system actually orbit the Sun). Mars proved the most elusive since, for Brahe's concept of the universe to be correct, it needed a much larger parallax than he could manage to record—a concept that was very difficult to grasp in the context of geocentrism.

Unfortunately for Brahe, who preferred to keep his observations and deductions within the grounds of Uraniborg, it seems that Wittich discussed their work with other scientists during a trip to Kassel in 1584.[37][A scientist in that city by the name of Nicolaus Reymers

---

[37] "Wittich (or Wittichius), Paul." *Complete Dictionary of Scientific Biography*. Web.

Bär (also called Reimarus Ursus) published a book four years later on the subject of prosthaphaeresis, in which parallaxial observations were used to propose a model of the universe in which Copernicus' and Ptolemy's theories were interlaced. It featured the Sun, Moon, and stars revolving around the Earth, while the other visible planets revolved around the Sun—a model that had clearly been influenced by Brahe's work.

Wittich never returned to Uraniborg after this dispute arose, though Brahe made efforts to remain on friendly terms. When the former died in 1586, Brahe focused his anger entirely on Reymers Bär for the usurpation of his work on prosthaphaeresis and the dual-centered universe, exonerating his friend for having played any role in the matter. Given Brahe's highly respected reputation as an astronomer, he did not face any insurmountable difficulty in gaining credit for his model of the universe—though, it was, of course, incorrect.

Paul Wittich may have been granted his due credit in contemporary times, but his name was not published alongside either Brahe's or Bär's as the author of the complex geo-helio-centric system. Therefore, after his death, his name eventually faded from the lips of the scientific community in Europe and almost disappeared from history altogether. His mathematical work, however, had advanced the subject of astronomy greatly and contributed to a large catalog of orbits and parallaxial distances between astral bodies and the Earth.

Chapter 10 – Sethus Calvisius

February 21, 1556–November 24, 1615

"...he not only attempts in this work to shew the errors of the Gregorian calendar, but offers also a new and more concise, as well as truer method of reforming the calendar."[38]

Sethus Calvisius (also known as either Setho Calvisio or Seth Kalwitz) was born in Germany to a poor family. He became a musician, and he was able to attend Magdeburg Gymnasium in 1572 and the Universities of Helmstedt (1589) and Leipzig (1580) to study music. He became the Director of Music at Pforten in 1582, and then in 1594, he became the Director of Music at Thomaskirche in Leipzig, where he remained until his death. While Calvisius was a musician, he was also an astronomer, a mathematician, and what was known as a chronologer (a person who studied historical records to establish dates of past events). Calvisius was actually offered several professorships as a mathematician at both Frankfurt and Wittenberg. But music was more important to Calvisius, and he kept to that for his main pursuit in life. He composed, taught, and wrote.

At that time, the "scientists" of the day were often philosophers and musicians. "Philosophy" was somewhat of a precursor to what we now consider a scientist. Calvisius is a prime example of a 16th- or a 17th- century philosopher or "thinker."

While his main efforts were in the musical realm, Calvisius spent a lot of time on astronomy. In 1605, Calvisius wrote about a system that he based on the records of around 300 astronomical eclipses to reckon historical events and create a chronology of them. He called it *Opus Chronologicum* (Chronological Work), and it was given support by some peers of his time.

The contributions to astronomical data collected and documented by Calvisius that was often used later by others is documented in a book

---

[38] "Sethus Calvisius (Germany; 1556–1615)." *1812 Chalmers' Biography*. Web.

called "The Story of Eclipses," written by George Frederick Chambers and first published in 1899.

> A vast amount of historical and other information respecting eclipses will be found in a book, the latinised name of whose author is Sethus Calvisius. The title of work is Opus Chronologicum. The historical matter is very much mixed, but the eclipses can be got hold of through the Index, which is very full.

Beyond his work with chronology, Calvisius worked on astronomical calculations that related to the Gregorian calendar. He created a new version of the calendar which he put forth in 1611 in his book called *Confutation of the Calendar, Approved and Established by Pope Gregory XIII*.[39] This work was meant to correct the Gregorian calendar which had been put into practice in 1582 and was considered an improvement from the Julian calendar as it calculated leap years in a better way. Calvisius' book meant to explain a truer method of calculating the calendar further, but his idea for reform was rejected. Calvisius continued to work on this project, as well as a corrected version of the book, but he did not live to publish it. It was published a few years after his death, however.

Calvisius' most lasting legacy to humanity is his music, and even to this day, you can hear his works performed.

---

[39] This was originally published in Latin in 1614 under the title *Formula calendarii novi*.

Chapter 11 – Joseph Goedenhuyze

?–1595

"By 1545, both Pisa and Padua had botanical gardens in which professors demonstrated plants to students...For the rest of the 16th century, scholars interested in the study of nature felt obliged to travel and study in Italy."[40]

Botany, or the study of plants, was of great interest in the 16th century, and much work was done to gather and study plants and their medicinal properties. Joseph Goedenhuyze (also known as Giuseppe Casabona) was a botanist who has been documented to have worked at just that. He was a Flemish man whose early life is unknown, but whose works have borne his signature for centuries after the man himself passed away.

What is known about Goedenhuyze is that he moved to Florence early on in life, probably around 1570, and came into the service of a nobleman named Niccolò Gaddi. Gaddi had extensive gardens, and soon, Goedenhuyze was traveling to the coast and the mountains to find new plants to document and bring back to nurture at Gaddi's palace and enrich his growing collection. Goedenhuyze's success

---

[40] Cambridge University Press et al. *The Cambridge History of Science Volume III.* 2003.

and enthusiasm for botany and Gaddi's standing in society soon brought notice to the botanical collections at Gaddi's gardens that thrived under the hand of Goedenhuyze.

In the late 16th century, Goedenhuyze was in the employ of Grand Duke Francesco I de' Medici and worked in his beautiful gardens, called the "Giardino Delle Stalle" and "Giardino dei Semplici." Goedenhuyze also worked in the garden at Casino di San Marco. In this position, Goedenhuyze was able to travel extensively throughout Italy in search of new plants for these high-profile gardens and those botanists and scientists interested in them. Unfortunately for the botanist, Francesco I's interest in his gardens waned toward the end of his life, and thus, his gardeners had less funding to continue studying and adding new specimens to the gardens. Upon his death, however, Francesco's successor, Ferdinand I de' Medici, stoked the interest in the gardens again and assured Goedenhuyze of his place there.

The Orto Botanico di Pisa was established in 1544 under Cosimo I de' Medici, and was the world's first botanical garden (Padua makes this claim as well, having been established in 1543 and because the garden at Pisa was later moved).[41,42] It was set up to be a research place for eminent botanists of the time.[43] Luca Ghini (1490–1556) was a prominent botanist whose research took place at these botanical gardens. Ghini installed an herbarium there in order to study herbs, and he was known to have dried specimens to study throughout the year rather than just during the growing season.

Joseph Goedenhuyze was appointed prefect (chief officer) of the Orto Botanico di Pisa and started there in 1592.[44] The gardens had

---

[43] Turner, T. *Italy Travel Guide*. 2019.

[44] Franco Bacchelli. "Goedenhuyze, Joseph', in Dizionario Biografico degli Italiani, Volume 57 (2001)." (in Italian.)

been moved, and he oversaw the moving of plants still in the old location to their new spot, which took about four years in total. Both the botanical gardens at Pisa and Padua are still extant today. This botanical garden has collections of seeds, specimens, scientific journals, and illustrations that are centuries old, and the work and dedication of Joseph Goedenhuyze have made a huge and lasting contribution to modern science.

Chapter 12 – Giordano Bruno

1548–February 17, 1600

"In space there are countless constellations, suns and planets; we see only the suns because they give light; the planets remain invisible, for they are small and dark. There are also numberless earths circling around their suns."[45]

Born in 1548 near Naples, Italy, Giordano Bruno (originally named Filippo Bruno) became a philosopher, astronomer, and mathematician whose theories often crossed into the occult.[46] His work was quite controversial and never accepted by the Catholic Church, whose constant harassment caused Bruno to move across the continent several times. During Bruno's lifetime, the Church was much more supportive of the Aristotelian model of the universe, in which the Earth was the central feature of the solar system. Proponents of theories outside of that norm were subjected at best to ridicule and at worst to torture and possibly death.

---

[45] Rees, Martin J. *Just Six Numbers: The Deep Forces that Shape the Universe.* 2000.
[46] Aquilecchia, Giovanni. "Giordano Bruno, Italian Philosopher." *Encyclopedia Britannica.* Web.

Bruno was perfectly aware of the particular scientific leanings of the Church since he studied theology within the Dominican Order in Naples, which is when he took the name Giordano. He was even ordained as a Catholic priest in 1572.[47] Despite his religious education and his position within the Catholic hierarchy, Bruno was spiritually unsatisfied with many facets of Christianity—and he was not shy about voicing his opinions. He was quite outspoken about his disbelief in the Holy Trinity, an integral feature of his own religion which stated God, Jesus, and the Holy Ghost are three separate pieces of the same ultimate divinity. Bruno rejected the idea that such a creature as God could become a human, thereby bridging the unbreachable gap between the divine and the mundane.

Bruno's impassioned grumblings against the doctrine of his own priesthood didn't go unnoticed, and a few years after earning his priestly robes, Bruno found himself at the center of a heresy investigation. Before the Italian Inquisition could call for his arrest, Bruno moved throughout Italy and France, before finally settling down in Geneva, Switzerland, for a brief time in 1579. There, he sought the company of the city's Calvinists, a Protestant denomination that adhered specifically to the philosophies of John Calvin.

Protestantism was sweeping throughout Europe thanks to the works of John Calvin, Martin Luther, and the Swiss philosopher Huldrych Zwingli. Each of these theologists and their proponents agreed on a few basic rules that differed from Catholic doctrine. One of the most controversial tenets of Protestantism was the belief that the bread and wine given during Holy Communion was not actually transformed into the body and blood of Christ during the ceremony. Protestants such as John Calvin and Martin Luther believed instead that the bread and wine were merely metaphorically representative of the body of Christ.

---

[47] Aquilecchia, Giovanni. "Giodano Bruno, Italian Philosopher." *Encyclopedia Britannica*. Web.

It isn't known whether Giordano Bruno actually became a Calvinist, though he did altogether abandon the Dominican Order. Though his evolving religious views may have had characteristics in common with Protestantism, Bruno's camaraderie with the Swiss Calvinists was probably based on their similar ongoing feud with Catholic Europe. Different interpretations of biblical details such as these were immensely important during the Middle Ages and the early modern era in Europe, as Giordano Bruno well knew. Even in the Calvinist haven of Geneva, he encountered serious criticism of his developing theologies. An attempt to receive a pardon for his heretical commentary from local representatives of the Catholic Church went badly, but Bruno still managed to find employment in Switzerland as a proofreader. Eventually, Bruno's outspokenness about his nonconformist beliefs placed him at the center of legal trouble again.

In August 1579, Bruno published a manuscript that harshly criticized the work of Antoine de la Faye, a French theologian and professor at the College of Geneva. Bruno's criticism led to his arrest as well as the book's publisher, and when they were released, Bruno left Switzerland for France. In 1580, he found employment as a professor of philosophy at the University of Toulouse. Bruno soon came under the patronage of Henry III, King of France, whose influence allowed him to passionately pursue his scientific theories of the universe without fear of repercussions.

According to Giordano Bruno,

> I got me such a name that King Henry III summoned me one day to discover from me if the memory which I possessed was natural or acquired by magic art. I satisfied him that it did not come from sorcery but from organised knowledge; and, following this, I got a book on memory printed, entitled *The Shadows of Ideas*, which I dedicated to His Majesty.

Forthwith he gave me an Extraordinary Lectureship with a salary.[48]

The Shadows of Ideas was not a theological work but instead a focused study of mnemonics. Memory-improvement techniques were another fundamental part of Bruno's scientific studies, and his complex memory wheel described in *The Shadows of Ideas* is still a part of modern university curriculum. The wheel is comprised of multiple layers of rings marked by Latin letters; to strengthen one's memory, one must memorize sequences of letters by assigning each a specific identity, action, or other details.

While in France, Bruno began once more to seriously pursue his astronomical studies. As before, he began with the Copernican heliocentric model of the universe. Copernicus himself had likely evaded torture and death at the hands of the authoritarian Church only because his natural death preceded the publication and sale of *De revolutionibus*. Unfortunately, Bruno had the unlucky fate to live contemporaneously alongside his own publications, including the highly controversial *De l'Infinito, Universo e Mondi* (or in English, *On the Infinite, Universe and Worlds*) published in 1584. By that time, he was living in London as the assistant of French Ambassador Michel de Castelnau. England was a Protestant country in which the Catholic Church no longer had any authority, and so, during his two and a half years there, Bruno wrote and published as many as eight books. His time in England was likely spent mostly in solitude, however, as his theories seemed to have not suitably impressed his English contemporaries.[49]

Where Copernicus' astronomical theory had ended, Bruno's began— and it kept right on going. Unaffected by a personal attachment to Church doctrine, the Italian astronomer let his collected data speak clearly and for itself. In *Infinite Universe*, he surmised that not only

---

[48] Boulting, William. *Giordano Bruno: His Life, Thought, and Martyrdom*. 1916.
[49] Feingold, Mordechai. "Giordano Bruno in England, Revisited." *Huntington Library Quarterly*. 2004.

did the Earth revolve around the Sun but that the universe was endless and altogether without a central feature. Furthermore, Bruno wondered if the stars he viewed in the night sky might be alien suns around which other planets revolved. If that were possible, Bruno wondered, then perhaps there may be alien forms of life inhabiting such planets.

Bruno's seemingly wild theories on astronomy and humankind's place in the universe were perhaps too outlandish for any contemporary audience, scholarly or otherwise. Europe was not ready for the Brunean model of the universe, in which there were multiple Earths, Suns, and potentially other forms of life. It was not only the clergy who resisted the idea but also other educated scientists of the age.

Upon his return to Italy as a mnemonics teacher in March 1592, Bruno was turned into the Italian Inquisition by none other than his own student. Bruno refused to bend to the whims of the Church, who ultimately arrested and charged him with heresy in May 1592 based on his religious beliefs. He was held and questioned in Venice, but as the trials continued, he was taken to Rome in February 1593. At that point, Bruno generally seemed to have been a non-Christian spiritualist who believed that God and Heaven were not separate from reality but perhaps a part of the physical world. He did not believe in the existence of Hell or the eternal damnation of the soul, nor did he find personal truth in the story of the divine Christ or the Virgin Mary. For Bruno, the journey of the soul involved reentry into the new body of a person or perhaps an animal. This was a major source of contention between Bruno and the Roman Inquisition, who incited a trial against him that lasted seven years.[50] Pope Clement VIII officially declared him a heretic on January 20, 1600, and Bruno was sentenced to death.[51] He was burned at the stake in Rome nearly a month later in a particularly brutal ceremony, hanging naked and upside-down.

---

[50] Davis, Daniel Paul. *Hysterically Historical: January II.* 2015.

Chapter 13 – Conrad Gessner

March 26, 1516–December 13, 1565

"In truth I rejoice and thank God because I have finally gotten out of the labyrinth in which I was trapped for almost three years. [This era has a] confusing and harmful abundance of books."[52]

Conrad Gessner was a Swiss scientist who was considered to be many things in the world of early science. He was a physician, a botanist, a zoologist, a philosopher, and even an illustrator, making him something of a "polymath," which is someone possessing wide-ranging knowledge.

Gessner's schooling was in theology, medicine, botany, and languages, for the most part, and he was sponsored by those who saw great hope in the young man who was too poor to attend school without financial assistance.

Gessner had a great interest in natural history, and he collected innumerable specimens from his travels and through contact with other scholars and friends. He kept detailed notes of the specimens he collected. One of the things that is thought to make Gessner stand

---

[51] Rowland, Ingrid D. *Giordano Bruno: Philosopher/Heretic.* 2016.
[52] Blair, Ann. "Reading strategies for coping with information overload, ca.1550-1700." *Journal of the History of Ideas,* 64, no. 1. 2003. 11-28.

out in this period of time is that rather than using the more standard method of relying on past writers for his research, he employed his own research. His methods of research included personal observation and accurate, detailed descriptions. He also used dissection to gain a better understanding of the specimens and to provide more detailed notes on them.

In 1551, Conrad Gessner published his *Historiae animalium* (or in English, *History of Animals*), and this book is considered to be the world's first version of an encyclopedia of all the known animals. This masterpiece ended up becoming a five-volume work with a complete bibliography of writings, and it is accepted as the first modern work of zoology. The volumes were published in Switzerland between 1551 and 1558.

Gessner's work on documenting the world's animals was so extensive that he included knowledge back to Aristotle's time, but he also worked to distinguish the difference between what was myth and what was fact. For this reason, his works included prehistoric and even mythical creatures, such as the unicorn. An excellent example of Gessner's reasoning on the unicorn gives great insight into his work:

> Horns are often discovered in Poland, and some people contend they are from the unicorn…on the grounds that each one is discovered separately, and two at a time has never been heard of, even though they have sometimes been found together with the very skull and the bones of the rest of the body…About five years ago Anton Schneeberger, once a student of mine, now a physician of great learning in eastern Poland, and foremost among thorough investigators of nature, wrote to me with a full and very careful account of this matter after he was allowed to see a number of such horns by means of my dearest friend Georg Joachim Rhaeticus, the most famous physician in eastern Poland at that time and a mathematician unrivalled in our age. "I saw that the first of these horns," he says, "was the length of my

outstretched arms, somewhat ash-gray or black in color, very sharp at the tip, smooth and round…The surface was flat, not turning in a spiral; its substance was crumbly, its shape curved. The inside was a very bright white color which acquired a dusky hue if it soaked up wine…This horn was found under the earth, no deeper than a foot, in a high and solitary place…by peasants digging to lay the foundation of a building…In fact, the whole animal was found, and it was larger than a horse, as is easily seen from the size of its bones. Based on the bones of the humeri, tibiae, and ribcage, it is certain that it was a quadruped…" Schneeberger also added that very many things of this sort are found in Poland, and therefore they are practically looked down on.[53]

Gessner's cataloging talents also targeted the world of plants between 1555 and 1565. This work, called *Historia Plantarum* (or in English, *History of Plants*), was not published during his life as he died of the plague in 1565. The book included about 1,500 illustrations of plants with detailed notations on them. The work was published quite sometime later in 1754.

Conrad Gessner's methodical and highly inclusive descriptions, drawings, research, and documentation were a huge example to the scientific world on methodology. He didn't merely record what a plant or animal looked like, but he also included any known history about it, complete physical descriptions, references to other sources of information about it, and as much data as he could gather on each and every specimen. He is attributed with being the first to describe some plants and animals, and later, many were even named after him.

---

[53] Gessner, C. *Icones animalium.* As translated by Erin Rushing in "Monoceros: What Conrad Gessner's discussion of the unicorn tells us about natural history in Renaissance Europe" *Smithsonian Libraries.* 2017.

He is considered by many to be the father of modern bibliography as well as a groundbreaking scientist in zoology and in botany.[54] In 1545, he wrote *Bibliotheca universalis*, in which he attempted to catalog all the known writing in Latin, Greek, and Hebrew. It contained about 12,000 titles, and it helped to contribute to Gessner's notorious opinion that contemporary society was simply overrun by literature.

Due to Gessner's Protestant religion, Pope Paul IV placed *History of Animals* on his extensive list of banned books in 1559.[55]

---

[54] Bay, Jens Christian. *Conrad Gesner (1516-1565), the Father of Bibliography: An Appreciation.* 2011.
[55] Birkhead, Tim. *The Wonderful Mr Willughby.* 2018.

Chapter 14 – Johannes Kepler

December 27, 1571–November 15, 1630

"We ought not to ask why the human mind troubles to fathom the secrets of the heavens. The diversity of the phenomena of nature is so great and the treasures hidden in the heavens so rich precisely in order that the human mind shall never be lacking in fresh nourishment."[56]

Johannes Kepler was born in the city of Weil der Stadt on December 27, 1571, which was located in a part of the Holy Roman Empire that would eventually become Germany. The boy and his siblings were raised in a household run by his mother and grandparents; his father had left the family to pursue a career as a mercenary soldier. Kepler proved to be a good student, and after he completed Latin school and Lutheran seminary studies in Adelberg, he earned a scholarship and was admitted to the University of Tübingen in September of 1589. Hoping to become a great thinker of the Church—known as a theologian—it turned out that the university preferred he undertake a teaching position because of his strength in mathematics. In a letter to his Tübingen mathematics professor in 1595, Kepler admitted that he had managed to find satisfaction in

---

[56] Kepler, Johannes, as quoted by Carl Sagan in *Cosmos*. 1980.

this work: "I wanted to become a theologian; for a long time I was restless. Now, however, behold how through my effort God is being celebrated in astronomy."[57]

Kepler was referring to the beauty he'd found in the patterns by which the planets he tracked across the sky were traveling. By studying those patterns and creating star maps, the astronomer concluded that all of God's creation—on and around the Earth—must be fundamentally geometric. He wrote of his findings and beliefs in the book *Mysterium Cosmographicum* (or in English, *The Cosmographic Mystery*), which was published in 1596. The book's major theory was that of Kepler's Platonic model of the universe. It was a complex model in which the relationships of the six known planets (Mercury, Venus, Earth, Mars, Jupiter, and Saturn) were defined by a series of geometric shapes. Those specific shapes had been described by the Greek philosopher Plato in the 5th century BCE, and therefore, Kepler called them the Platonic solids.

Four years after publishing *Mysterium*, Kepler became the astronomical assistant to none other than Tycho Brahe. Kepler and Brahe had first met in February of 1600, and Brahe was suitably impressed with his colleague's recent book. They began their work together in a place near Prague, and Kepler was assigned to study the orbit of Mars. Apparently, Brahe was quite a strict master, as he wouldn't allow his assistant to look at his vast collection of data and research, much of which had been compiled from the notes of Copernicus. Kepler was meant to focus on Mars and otherwise only do as he was told. The key to the treasures was the death of the master himself, which came to pass just a short time later in 1601.

Brahe was 54 at the time of his death, which modern physicians have concluded probably was caused by uremia—a condition in which the blood contains toxic levels of urea. According to Johannes Kepler, Brahe had caused his own demise eleven days before dying by refusing to break etiquette during a banquet in Prague. Instead of

---

[57] Bradstreet, David Hart. *Star Struck.* 2016.

leaving the table to urinate, Brahe stayed put and probably burst his bladder.[58] The escaping urine poisoned his blood and led to an excruciating illness that ended on October 24, 1601.[59]

For Kepler, Brahe's passing meant that the former lord of Uraniborg's data all passed to him. Unfortunately, Uraniborg itself was completely destroyed shortly after the death of Brahe by the King of Denmark, Christian IV. Christian inherited his father's crown in 1588 at the age of eleven.[60] Too young to rule yet, he relied on a regency council that continued funding Brahe's palatial scientific research center for many years. When Christian IV came of age in 1596, however, he revoked all funding and set Brahe adrift.[61]

After the lord of Uraniborg died, Kepler succeeded him as the new imperial mathematician to the Holy Roman Emperor, Rudolph II. It was a position he held for eleven years and one in which he received adequate funding to continue his research—albeit perhaps not in such a perfect laboratory as Brahe's had been. Thanks to Brahe's extensive catalogs of planetary motion, Kepler was able to solidify his three laws of motion:

1. All planets move about the Sun in elliptical orbits, having the Sun as one of the foci.

2. A radius vector joining any planet to the Sun sweeps out equal areas in equal lengths of time.

3. The squares of the sidereal periods (the time it takes for a planet to complete one revolution in respect to the fixed

---

[58] Tierney, John. "Murder! Intrigue! Astronomers?" *New York Times*. November 29, 2010.

[59] Eggin, Olin Jeuck. "Tycho Brahe, Danish Astronomer." *Encyclopedia Britannica*. Web.

[60] Bain, Robert Nisbet. "Christian IV." *Encyclopedia Britannica*. Web.

[61] Ibid.

stars) of the planets are directly proportional to the cubes of their mean distances from the Sun.[62]

All of this could have been confidently calculated despite the shortcomings of Brahe's universal model since all planets, except Earth, had been correctly identified as orbiting the Sun. These were significant rudiments for the study of physics, and yet these laws of motion were by no means Kepler's only discoveries. He was also very interested in the field of optics, and after the invention of the telescope by German-Dutch optician Hans Lippershey (1570–1619) in 1608, that interest became the focus of a series of experiments.[63]

In *Astronomiae Pars Optica* (or in English, *The Optical Part of Astronomy*), published in 1604, Kepler speculated upon the process of vision within the eye, experimenting with pinhole cameras and glass lenses to decipher how light enters the eye and refracts within it to form a picture. He used the data from these experiments to create corrective eyeglass lenses for both myopia and hyperopia, and he posited that the parallax created by our two front-facing eyes creates a fundamental perception of depth. He tried to use that same principle to calculate the distance between the stars, but their width was too minute for measuring devices of the day.

It wasn't until 1605 that Kepler finally understood that the orbit of the planet he'd been studying closely since starting work with Tycho Brahe, Mars, was elliptical, not circular.[64] The circle, considered a majestic and perfect path for all celestial bodies, was at the foundation of all contemporary astronomical work, and therefore, Kepler's realization that planets did not necessarily move in circles was incredibly important. The elliptical orbit of Mars, as described

---

[62] "Kepler's laws of planetary motion. Astronomy." *Encyclopedia Britannica.* Web.

[63] Cox, Lauren. "Who invented the telescope?" *Space.com.* Web. 21 December 2017.

[64] Lambert, Tim. "A short biography of Johannes Kepler." *Local Histories.* Web.

by Kepler, would allow future scientists to more accurately map the movement of bodies in our solar system.

Once Kepler's contemporary Galileo Galilei finetuned Lippershey's invention for detailed stargazing, Kepler extended his own lens-work to include telescopic observations. Kepler was intrigued by the physicality of the telescope and how it could best be put together. His next book, *Dioptrice*, published in 1611, explained how a telescope worked and described the differences in the types of images produced by them.

In 1614, Kepler published *De Vero Anno quo Aeternus Dei Filius Humanam Naturam in Utero Benedictae Virginis Mariae Assumpsit* (*Concerning the True Year in Which the Son of God Assumed a Human Nature in the Uterus of the Blessed Virgin Mary*), an important Christian science document that chronologically placed the birth of Jesus in 4 BCE, five years prior to the accepted date. This theory would come to be almost universally accepted, though contemporary calendar changes into the Gregorian style would not address those lost five years.

His 1615 book, *Nova stereometria doliorum vinariorum*, formed the basis of integral calculus, a form of mathematics that focuses on the area or volume of objects. The topic struck him suddenly during preparations for his marriage to his second wife (his first wife had passed away in 1611) to Susanna Reuttinger in 1613. While haggling over the price of a barrel of wine with a merchant, Kepler realized that the traditional method used to calculate the volume of such a barrel might be flawed; this led to his own experiments in such calculations, and the title of the book, which translates to *New Solid Geometry of Wine Barrels*.[65]

The vendor for Kepler's wedding used a long rod, inserted into a hole halfway down the length of the barrel, to measure the volume of

---

[65] Cardil, Roberto. "Kepler: The volume of a wine barrel." *Convergence*. January 2012.

the object. The longer the length of rod that fit into the barrel from this point, called the "bunghole," the higher the volume of the barrel. As a savvy mathematician, Kepler, of course, knew that cylinders with radically different volumes might give the same results with such methodology. He, therefore, attempted to find a better way to measure volume, starting with a series of triangles to fill the area of a circle, which was then duplicated and stacked to replicate a barrel. Though many of Kepler's calculations were quite precise, he struggled to mathematically represent the curvature of both the circle and the barrel.

Kepler's keen observations of the physical world also lent themselves to the oceanic tides, which he believed could be explained by forces of attraction between the water and the Moon, as well as the water and the Earth. He postulated that it was this attraction that caused the immense bodies of water upon the Earth to move back and forth between the two attractive forces. This was not a popular theory at the time; nevertheless, it was correct, and Kepler seems to have been the first European scientist to believe in it.

At this point in time, Kepler was no longer working under Emperor Rudolf but rather his successor, Matthias, and in 1619, he continued his work under Holy Roman Emperor Ferdinand II. Johannes Kepler enjoyed a reasonably lengthy career and very little backlash from detractors, especially from those within the Catholic and Protestant Churches. As the imperial mathematician, his position was not only highly respected but prone to little criticism. Unfortunately, Kepler's personal beliefs conflicted with that of his Catholic patron, and after a little over a decade serving as the lead scientist to the Holy Roman Emperors Rudolph II, Matthias, and Ferdinand II, Kepler left the position. Life became more complicated afterward since Kepler's Protestantism caused him no end of trouble.

During the Thirty Years' War, caused mostly by the failings of Holy Roman Emperors Rudolf II and Matthias but perpetuated by Ferdinand's need to restore Catholicism to the Holy Roman Empire, Protestants were actively hunted and punished in Roman Catholic dominions. Kepler, his family members, and millions of other Europeans were forced to flee their homes multiple times to avoid the emperor's armies, as well as riots and individual zealots. At one point, the scientist was forced to defend his mother at a witchcraft trial. She was spared, but the family spent the rest of their lives moving from city to city, trying to stay ahead of the Inquisition.

He died in Regensburg, Germany, in 1630 in poverty.[66] His accounts had been frozen by the Catholic authorities, and he'd fallen ill while traveling from his home in Sagan, Poland, to collect a debt repayment. His grave was soon destroyed in the tumult of the ongoing Thirty Years' War, but Kepler had taken the fields of astronomy, physics, and mathematics a considerable distance in terms of practical theory. He wrote his own epitaph, which survives to this day and reads: "I used to measure the heavens, now I measure the shadows of Earth. Although my mind was heaven-bound, the shadow of my body lies here."[67]

---

[66] Voelkel, James R. *Johannes Kepler: And the New Astronomy.* 2001.

[67] Krantz, Steven G. and Brian E. Blank. *Calculus: Multivariable.* 2006.

Chapter 15 – Daniel Sennert

November 25, 1572–July 21, 1647

"[I]t is a very simple substance or a certain spiritus, in which the soul and the plastic force immediately reside, and contains within itself the Idea of the organic body from which it has fallen, thus possesses the potentiality both to form an organic body similar to that from which it has fallen to prefect itself into an individual of the same species as [that] *of the parent."*[68]

Daniel Sennert was the son of a shoemaker in what is now Poland. He was an educated man who earned a master's degree in 1598 from the University of Wittenberg in Germany and then a medical degree in 1601.[69] After graduation, he became a professor at that university. He was a prolific writer and authored several books that dealt with chemistry and alchemy between 1611 and 1636. Some of Sennert's writings are still available today, such as *Meditations Upon Living Holily and Dying Happily (with Suitable Prayers to Each Chapter)*. His original writings were in Latin, but many were translated and can still be found in modern reprints.

---

[68] Sennert, Daniel, quoted by Hiro Hirai in *Medical Humanism*. 2011.
[69] "Sennert, Daniel." *The Galileo Project*. Web. 1995.

In Sennert's early scientific work, he did not subscribe much to the theory of alchemy, but in later years, he began to incorporate it as proven fact. At that time in history, alchemy and chemistry were both considered scientific even though alchemy embraced within it a supernatural element that chemistry omitted.

Daniel Sennert's work contributed to an early type of atomic theory which proposed that matter was made from atoms. Most notably, Sennert's work connected the work of alchemists and corpuscularianism, which was the theory that matter was made of smaller particles. Though his theories on the subject of matter would eventually be proven correct, it would take more than two centuries for atomic theory to find its place within the foundations of chemistry.

Daniel Sennert was among those intellectuals of his day promoting the use of "antiscorbutics"[70] to cure scurvy and other ailments.[71] Lemon juice became the main cure for scurvy, and other herbal mixtures were also created, although many of those were later found to be ineffective as they did not actually contain enough Vitamin C.

Sennert's work as a physician and scientist contributed some important practical advances to humanity in the field of medicine. He identified and documented an outbreak of scarlatina (scarlet fever) that helped in the study of the illness. He also made significant additions to what was known about dysentery and scurvy. At that time, it was not known how dysentery came to infect people and whether it was contagious, and Sennert was able to narrow down the causes of the illness and show adequate evidence of its contagious characteristics.[72] His work on dysentery from the 17th

---

[70] "Antiscorbutic" as defined by the *Oxford English Dictionary:* "(chiefly of a drug) having the effect of preventing or curing scurvy."

[71] Hughes, Elwyn. "The Rise and Fall of the 'Antiscorbutics': Some Notes on the Traditional Cures for 'Land Scurvy'." *Medical History.* 1990.

[72] Woodward, Joseph. *The Medical and Surgical History of the War of the Rebellion.* 1879.

century was still being referred to with great significance in further works in the 19th century. The knowledge that there were particles in the body that were causing illnesses helped advance the work in how to fight them, whether they were from bacteria or from a virus.

Sennert's work on particles and disease in the mid-1600s was quite thorough and advanced the fight against diseases considerably. At one point, he described the cause of high temperatures during what were called "putrid fevers" as "sharp particles."[73] His book *Practical Physick* dealt with:

> Practical physick, or, Five distinct treatises of the most predominant diseases of these times : the first of the scurvy, the second of the dropsie, the third of feavers and agues of all sort, the fourth of the French pox, and the fifth of the gout, wherein the nature, causes, symptoms, various methods of cure, and waies of preventing every of the said diseases, are severally handled, and plainly discovered to the meanest capacity.

This book provided great insight and information to physicians and scientists of the day who were dealing with some of the most devastating illnesses and diseases.

Between 1611 and 1636, Sennert worked on hypotheses about atomic structures. He believed that the previous work of many authors proved that iron could be changed to copper, and so, he based his work on that belief, which was, of course, later proven to be false.

Sennert stated that medicine and chemistry must discover the laws of nature as they are a part of a single knowledge rather than separate pieces. One of his most well-known experiments dealt with what is known as the "reduction to the pristine state," which goes back to Aristotle's time. The original experiment reduces a gold and silver

---

[73] Bynum, W.F. and Nutton, V., *Theories of Fever from Antiquity to the Enlightenment.* 1981.

alloy then removes the silver and puts it back into its original state. Sennert's experiment went further and filtered the silver that was removed, showing that there were remaining tiny particles of the substance, which furthered the theory of corpuscularianism. Sennert's discovery with this experiment is thought to have inspired further work on atomic theory by other scientists such as Robert Boyle.

Daniel Sennert lived in Wittenberg until his death in 1647, which was due to the plague.

Chapter 16 – Galileo Galilei

February 15, 1564– January 8, 1642

"I wish, my dear Kepler, that we could have a good laugh together at the extraordinary stupidity of the mob. What do you think of the foremost philosophers of this University? In spite of my oft-repeated efforts and invitations, they have refused, with the obstinacy of a glutted adder, to look at the planets or Moon or my telescope."[74]

Once again from the Duchy of Florence, a polymath appeared, this time in 1564 and by the name of Galileo Galilei. Encouraged by his father to attend the University of Pisa and join the medical field, young Galileo, instead, found himself transfixed on the study of physical objects and their movements. He switched his studies to mathematics and natural sciences, and as a result, he became one of the most important astronomers and physicists of his time. Perhaps his longest-lasting contribution to science was the further development of an existing piece of technology—the telescope—into astronomy's most important tool.

In fact, many people believed (and still do) that Galileo invented the telescope—it was, of course, not his invention but a constant work of scientific innovation. Whereas Lippershey's original telescope

---
[74] Plottner, Tammy. *The Night Sky Companion.* 2009.

consisted of two lenses and presented an upside-down image to the observer, Galileo experimented with different types of lenses to further magnify objects in view and switch the final image right-side-up. The housing for the lenses was a tube constructed of wooden strips, and there was a strip of leather around the eyepiece. The instrument was 92.7 centimeters in length (36.50 inches) and a width of 37 millimeters (1.5 inches).[75] The viewing hole was only 2 millimeters (.08 inches) in diameter, so, therefore, the telescope—contemporarily called a spyglass or optical tube—could only cover a very tiny piece of the sky.[76] Nevertheless, it magnified the view eight times, and after a few months of experimenting, Galileo's later telescopes could magnify as much as thirty times.

The telescopes for which he became famous were constructed with a biconcave lens at the eyepiece and a planoconvex lens within the instrument. Because of the shapes of these delicate pieces of glass, as well as the distance between them, higher magnification was within reach than had been possible with Lippershey's single-sided (encompassing both convex and concave curves) lenses. Galileo was so determined to fine-tune Lippershey's invention that he began grinding and polishing the glass lenses himself to achieve his own exacting standards.

Using his telescope, Galileo looked up at the Moon, of which he could only view about one quarter at a time. He was excited to discover that the surface of the Moon was not smooth, as had been assumed, but that it was covered in pockmarks, hills, and valleys. It was to be the first major astronomical discovery of many. Using his later 30-magnification telescope, Galileo was also able to observe the planets of our solar system. It was January 7, 1610, when he first laid eyes on three small stars surrounding Jupiter.[77] Though one lay

---

[75] "Galileo´s telescope." *Virtual Museum, Museo Galileo.* Web. 2015.

[76] Ibid.

[77] Plotner, Tammy. "What is Galileo's Telescope?" *Universe Today.* Web. 13 July 1016.

to the west of Jupiter and the others to the east, the following night Galileo found all three stars to the west of the planet. Soon, he noticed a fourth member of the group, and Galileo realized that he had not found stars but a collection of moons orbiting Jupiter. These were Io, Ganymede, Callisto, and Europa.

By turning his creations toward Venus, Galileo also was able to document the phases of that planet. They were much like those of the Moon, which suggested Venus orbited around the Sun, not the Earth—a theory posited both by Tycho Brahe, Nicolaus Copernicus, and Johannes Kepler. Evidence that the Earth was not the center of the universe continued to pile up, and it included the discoveries of two more planets: Venus and Neptune. Galileo also realized that the Milky Way was a collection of stars and not something analogous to a cloud.

Galileo, though his own work was highly praised by Johannes Kepler, did not agree with the latter that the Moon was responsible for producing oceanic tides. Instead, Galileo believed that the tides were caused by the movement of the Earth around the Sun, as well as the rotation of the Earth upon its axis. It would eventually turn out that Kepler had this one right, however; though Galileo's perfectly heliocentric model of the universe would prove to be correct. It was a modified version of the Copernican universe.

As always, heliocentrism without the Earth positioned at the Sun's side was controversial. In fact, Pope Paul V formally declared to be in favor of the geocentric universe in the early 17th century, but his personal friendship with Galileo Galilei kept the latter out of political harm.[78] Though Galileo was somewhat protected from backlash, the pope banned Copernicus' *De revolutionibus* in 1616 and instructed Galileo that the Copernican theory could not be taught as fact.[79] However, Galileo was allowed to continue his studies in search of evidence and use the geocentric model as a theoretical

---

[78] "Geocentrism." *Scripture Catholic*. Web.

device. That same year, Galileo was assured by the pope that as long as he was in office, Galileo would be safe from religious persecution due to his scientific theories. Eager for proof of such a promise, Galileo requested and received an official letter stating his permission from the Church to teach both geocentrism and heliocentrism as theories. The letter was issued by Cardinal Bellarmine.

Paul V died in 1621, and he was succeeded for a short time by Pope Gregory XV, who was then succeeded by Pope Urban VIII, the latter of which had no patience for the Copernican theory touted by Galileo.[80] Though Urban VIII was willing to let Galileo's dual-model comparisons continue as before, the latter published *Dialogue Concerning the Two Chief World Systems* in 1632 and lost all papal support. In *Dialogue*, a character called Simplicio (a name connoted with a simpleton) tediously argued for the Ptolemaic, geocentric model of the universe. The other characters in the book, staunch Copernicans, ridiculed Simplicio. It was obvious that the author found non-Copernican models outdated and incorrect, and in crafting his dialogues as he did, Galileo seemed to personally ridicule the pope, whether that was truly his intention or not. Pope Urban VIII had *Dialogues* banned from further sale and brought it before the Catholic Inquisition for inspection.

In 1633, Galileo was charged with heresy for teaching the Copernican theory, in which the Earth did not lay at the center of all things and that it moved—theories that opposed the biblical version of a fixed Earth at the center of the universe. Galileo presented his letter from Cardinal Bellarmine, but it was of little use. The scientist was found guilty of heresy on June 22, 1633, and he was sentenced to imprisonment.[81] Ownership of *Dialogue* was banned outright, but Galileo was ultimately allowed to serve his imprisonment as a term

---

[79] "Vatican Bans Copernicus' Book." *Physics Today.* Web. 5 March 2015.
[80] "Paul V, pope." *Encyclopedia Britannica.* Web.

[81] Hacket Publishing. *The Trial of Galileo: Essential Documents.* 2014.

of house arrest in the home of Archbishop Piccolomini. Having been a well-mannered house guest with Piccolomini, Galileo was eventually allowed to return to his own home in Arcetri, near Florence, but remained unable to leave the grounds. He lived there for the rest of his life, dying at the age of 77.

Chapter 17 – William Harvey

April 1, 1578–June 3, 1657

"The heart of animals is the foundation of their life, the sovereign of everything within them, the sun of their microcosm, that upon which all growth depends, from which all power proceeds."[82]

William Harvey took it upon himself to produce a similar work to his contemporary, Andreas Vesalius, except that his dissections were performed largely on animals. An English physician, Harvey had studied medicine in Italy before returning to England to practice his vocation. He was particularly interested in how blood flowed through the body, and he made great efforts to untangle the mystery of the circulatory system. His research also centered heavily upon the heart, and he realized that this was the pumping system by which blood moved through the vessels of the body.

In 1628, Harvey published his findings in *Exercitatio Anatomica de Motu Cordis et Sanguinis in Animalibus* (or in English, *An Anatomical Exercise on the Motion of the Heart and Blood in Living Beings*). The book revolutionized anatomical and medical knowledge about blood, specifically in that Harvey's research

---

[82] Harvey, William. *An Anatomical Disquisition on the Motion of the Heart and Blood in Animals*. 1628.

showed solid support for his theory that a fixed amount of blood circulated throughout the body. He included measurements whenever possible, observing that two ounces of blood left the heart with each beat. Given an average of 72 beats per minute for an adult, that would equate to 540 pounds of blood moving through the body every hour. Harvey immediately realized that was an insupportable amount of blood for humans whose weight averaged some 300 pounds less than the estimated mass of blood. Therefore, he postulated, there must be one body of blood being pumped out of the heart and eventually returning from whence it came. If blood was pumped out of the heart, he theorized, and into the arteries, it must return via the blood vessels to complete a closed circuit. Harvey's theory was consistent with the evidence he found since blood vessels contained one-way valves.

Harvey's personal life was no less exciting than his professional one. In 1604, he married Elizabeth Browne, the daughter of the royal physician Lancelot Browne.[83] Lancelot Browne had served as a physician to Queen Elizabeth I before her death in 1603, and before his own death just two years later, he performed the same service for the queen's successor, King James I. Harvey's marital connection to the Browne family helped solidify his own place in English medicine, and he was made a Fellow of the Royal College of Physicians in 1607.[84]

Harvey was awarded a great opportunity in 1615 when the Royal College of Physicians appointed him the new Lumleian Lecturer.[85] The regular lecture series had begun in 1582 when Lord John Lumley and physician Richard Caldwell founded surgical lectures for the college's students.[86] In 1616, Harvey began his own series of

---

[83] "William Harvey (1578 – 1657.)" *BBC History*. Web. 2014.

[84] Gregory, Andrew. "William Harvey, English Physician." *Encyclopedia Britannica*. Web.

[85] Ibid.

[86] Burns, William E. *The Scientific Revolution: An Encyclopaedia*. 2001.

talks focused on the circulatory system, and although he had already made his own conclusions about the path blood takes through the body, he only revealed this information to his audience over the course of several years. His lectures were accompanied by dissections, in which he was determined to display the total contents of the body to his students. Harvey demanded that his students display the utmost respect for each other during his lectures, clearly stating that students were never to boldly contradict one another.

Following in the footsteps of his father-in-law, Harvey himself became the new physician to the first King of England and Scotland in 1618, James I.[87] The new job was incredibly prestigious but probably a little terrifying as well, since one of Harvey's predecessors, Doctor Roderigo Lopez, had been drawn and quartered after being found guilty of attempting to poison Queen Elizabeth I.

Fortunately, Harvey was on excellent terms with King James, and then with his successor, King Charles I, who received the crown in 1625.[88] Charles I and Harvey lived in England during a violent and chaotic time of civil war, and ultimately, the king was deposed and forced to give up his monarchic rights under the influence of his powerful Puritan detractor, Oliver Cromwell. While the Cromwell government was in power, Harvey fled London alongside Charles I, while the Puritans collected and destroyed many of the physician's research notes at his home. His friend and patron headed up the royal armies for years before becoming imprisoned on the Isle of Wight. Harvey stayed away from the nation's capital until 1647, having no king and no family to return to since he and Elizabeth had had no children and Elizabeth had died years earlier. [89] Two years later, King Charles I was executed, and England was declared a commonwealth state.

---

[87] "William Harvey (1578 – 1657.)" *BBC History*. Web. 2014.

[88] "Charles I (r.1625-1649.)" *Royal.uk*. Web.

[89] Gregory, Andrew. "William Harvey, English Physician." *Encyclopedia Britannica*. Web.

Harvey claimed to have lost a valuable entomological manuscript at the hands of Cromwell's men, as well as notes on the circulatory system. He retired from treating patients upon his return to London but did continue to lecture at the Royal College of Physicians. He also proceeded to publish *Exercitationes de generatione animalium* (or in English, *On Animal Generation*), a precursor to modern embryology, in 1651. Harvey's unwavering interest in the anatomy of animals and humans led him and others to a greater understanding of the mammalian body than ever before. In *Exercitationes*, he was the first scientist to theorize that mammals—including humans—produced offspring due to a process of fertilization of an egg by sperm. In the years preceding the development of a powerful microscope, Harvey's theories on mammalian eggs were impossible to prove, but it still intrigued the scientific community.

William Harvey died of a stroke in 1657.[90] Just four years later, Italian anatomist Marcello Malpighi made a demonstration of the body's capillary circulation, definitively proving Harvey's theory about the circulation of the blood.[91]

---

[90] Silverman, Mark E. "De Motu Cordis: the Lumleian Lecture of 1616." *Journal of the Royal Society of Medicine.* 2007.

[91] Ibid.

Chapter 18 – René Descartes

March 31, 1596–February 11, 1650

"If you would be a real seeker after truth, it is necessary that at least once in your life you doubt, as far as possible, all things." [92]

Like their intellectual idols, the ancient Greeks and Romans, Europeans during the Scientific Revolution also had a deep respect for the intangible science of philosophy. René Descartes, a French mathematician and scientist, also spent a great deal of his time philosophizing, and it was for the latter pursuit he would mostly be remembered. His work often provided a link between the physical sciences and philosophy, particularly in terms of developing a firm scientific method.

Born in the Kingdom of France, Descartes' family was Roman Catholic. The Le Haye en Touraine region, however, was under the rule of Calvinists whom the French called Huguenots. They would later come under violent and bloody oppression due to the Catholic Church in the latter part of the 17th century, but during Descartes' childhood, there was a relative accord between the two parties. Young Descartes attended a Catholic Jesuit school in La Fléche

---

[92] Descartes, Rene. *Principia philosophiae.* 1644.

before moving on to the University of Poitiers and earning his licence (the French equivalent of a degree) in canon and civil law.

After obtaining his qualifications to practice law, Descartes moved to Paris and gave very little further thought to formal education or even the habits of reading and writing. For two years, the young man socialized with diverse groups and learned what he could of the world before joining the Protestant Dutch States Army as a private mercenary in 1618.[93] Under the tutelage of the army, he learned military engineering and became acquainted with the Dutch philosopher Isaac Beeckman. Beeckman and Descartes found a shared fondness for mathematics, and together, they worked on the problem of linking mathematics to the field of physics. The very next year, Descartes woke from a series of dreams in which he believed a divine spirit revealed how all the truths of science and math were linked together. From then on, he believed that his life's work was to find those links.

The various scientific fields were, in Descartes' day, filled with hobbyists and professionals alike, and both of those created flawed experiments that served to prove their personal hypotheses; the problem with this approach is that it conforms to personal bias. "Confirmation bias," as a psychological term, was not used until the mid-20th century by Peter Wason, but Descartes could still see its influence on the world of science.[94] Confirmation bias is the tendency of an observer to search for evidence that supports their own belief—for example, if a biological researcher studying the human brain believed Africans to be intellectually inferior to other

---

[93] Bruno, Leonard C. *Math and Mathematicians: The History of Math Discoveries Around the World.* 2003.

[94] Klein, Gary, Ph.D. "The Curious Case of Confirmation Bias." *Psychology Today.* Web. May 5, 2019.

members of the human race, he might unconsciously choose small African skulls to examine or measure those samples incorrectly.[95]

Descartes believed that we should attempt to keep our assumptions to ourselves. No scientific report or experiment should be given merit just on the basis of the scientist to prove his own point, Descartes argued. Instead, hypotheses should be proven through a chain of reasoning and exposed to elements that may altogether disprove them. In fact, Descartes was so skeptical of the supposed realities of science that he was loath to commit himself to any particular belief or conclusion. He famously wrote, "I think, therefore I am," which means that because Descartes was able to think, he knew he existed, but he was hesitant to assume anything else.[96]

Descartes wanted his work to be read by all his fellow Frenchmen, so he forewent the typical Latin treatise on his subject and published it in French. The *Discourse on the Method of Rightly Conducting One's Reason and of Seeking Truth in the Sciences* outlined the benefits of deductive reasoning, a methodology that was closely linked to the author's education in law. Descartes posited that conclusions about any idea or object could only be drawn once all doubt had been removed. If one time out of ten trials an experiment had unexpected results, then solid conclusions could not be drawn. Experiments should be repeatable; otherwise, they must be disregarded. The book laid out four primary pillars of scientific methodology:

1. Do not accept anything as truth until all reasonable doubt has been removed.

2. Break large problems into smaller problems.

3. Document all knowledge of the problem, starting with simple facts and ascending to the more complex information.

---

[95] This exact experiment was conducted by Samuel George Morton, and its results published between 1839 and 1849.

[96] Descartes. *Discourse on the Method.* 1637.

4. Make all explanations so detailed and complete that nothing can be missed.

Though Descartes is generally remembered for his contribution to scientific methodology, he was also a brilliant mathematician. He found satisfaction in mathematical studies from an early age, largely because of the regimented methods and sound, complete answers involved. Working specifically with geometry and algebra, Descartes created the new field of analytical geometry to link them together. Using his own advice from *Method*, Descartes figured out complex, unsolvable geometry problems by breaking them into smaller parts and expressing them algebraically. To bring horizontal and vertical information from these problems into a more tangible light, he created the algebraic graph, in which the vertical dimension is represented by y and the horizontal dimension is represented by x. These graphs are used daily in modern classrooms.

His great work on physical science, entitled *Le Monde, ou Traité de la Lumière*, was kept from publishing houses for many years, and it was only printed in its entirety after his death. The title translated into English is "The World, or Treatise on the Light." In these pages, Descartes described a heliocentric universe in which all the parts were made of tiny particles. Every object in the universe was in constant motion, which kept all the parts from crashing into one another in what he believed was a vacuum-less void. Descartes most likely delayed the book's release in 1633 due to Galileo Galilei being sentenced to imprisonment for his work citing the Sun as the center of the universe instead of the Earth.

Chapter 19 – Margaret Cavendish

1623–December 15, 1673

"I am not covetous, but as ambitious as ever any of my sex was, is, or can be; which makes, that though I cannot be Henry the Fifth, or Charles the Second, yet I endeavour to be Margaret the First."[97]

Margaret Lucas was born into a privileged English family in 1623. She was tutored at home but not formally educated; her brother John, however, had the good fortune to receive a formal secondary education, and his interests in science and philosophy caught the attention of Margaret. As a young woman, Margaret would rely on topics of science and literature to entertain her throughout the English Civil War, during which she was exiled in Paris.

Given her aristocratic background, Margaret was able to find employment at the English royal court of King Charles I and his wife, Queen Henrietta Maria, before the civil war broke out. Once the fighting began, though, the monarchs were forced into hiding, and since Margaret was loyal to her employers, she left England at the side of the queen. Living in exile from 1644 until the mid-1650s, Margaret met and married another English royalist in Paris: William Cavendish.

Though William Cavendish was unable to return to England during the Commonwealth period, his wife could do so whenever she chose.

---

[97] Cavendish, Margaret. *The Blazing World.* 1666.

At the time, English lawmakers under the authority of Thomas Cromwell, Lord Protector of England, required any expatriates to renounce their loyalty to the royal family upon returning to England. Cavendish was unwilling to do so, but Margaret wasn't required to make any such oath. Ironically, due to her status as a female and therefore being a secondary citizen of England, Margaret's political beliefs were of no importance to the administration. Therefore, she traveled back and forth between England and France quite freely.

During these trips to England, she had her various poems, stories, and philosophical essays published.

Chapter 20 – Robert Boyle

January 25, 1627–December 31, 1691

"It is my intent to beget a good understanding between the chymists and the mechanical philosophers who have hitherto been too little acquainted with one another's learning."[98]

At the age of eight, Robert Boyle entered the prestigious English preparatory school, Eton College. As the son of an aristocratic Irish father, Boyle enjoyed the best education any British boy could hope for. He even had a private tutor, Isaac Marcombes, who accompanied him and his brother on a grand tour of Europe. Though Robert's older brother was sent home early to join his family during the Irish Rebellion of 1642, Robert stayed in Geneva with Marcombes. Two years later, at the age of 23, he went to England and began a literary career.

Boyle was initially concerned with ethics and rhetoric, but after a decade of examining and philosophizing on French literature, he became interested in natural philosophies. In the 1650s, he began spending a great deal of time with the Hartlib Circle, a group of

---

[98] Boyle, Robert. *The Sceptical Chymist.* 1661.

intellectuals that was centered on the educator Samuel Hartlib. Among the members of the Hartlib Circle were a few experimental scientists whose work enthralled Robert Boyle.

Boyle's personal relationships with scientists who dedicated their time to conducting hands-on experiments inspired him to design and conduct his own. A great deal of data upon which the Scientific Revolution depended was compiled through experiments that looked at the world on a much smaller scale than ever before. Just as physicians needed to look inside their specimens to learn about the organs and tiny vessels that made up an animal, so, too, did Robert Boyle change the scales in his pursuit of knowledge of chemistry.

Through a series of experiments, Boyle realized that the volume of a gas decreases with increasing pressure and increases with decreasing pressure. For a specific mass of gas, Boyle discovered that the pressure multiplied by the volume of that gas equaled a constant, nearly unchanging number. This relationship is called Boyle's law.[99] The discovery that gases acted in such a way prompted Boyle to consider how such behavior might be possible, and to answer his own questions, Boyle had to think about gas as a collection of tiny, invisible particles. It was still in the early days for the microscope, and even the strongest lens could not see the particles of gas Boyle was working with. Boyle's hypothesis on the structure of atoms and molecules was entirely theoretical and based on a type of scientific model.

The scientific model is an important part of modern science, though it has no specific shape; its purpose is to give the scientist a more comprehensive way to think about the subject at hand. For theories about physical elements that cannot be directly observed, such as the movement of gases, a scientific model allows the scientist and others to visualize what is happening. For example, since Robert Boyle was working with invisible gases, his own scientific model of such gases was a visual representation of a collection of tiny particles that

---

[99] "Boyle's Law." *Science History Institute.* Web. 1 December 2017.

comprise a gas. Like the theory of corpuscularianism, Boyle's interpretation of his experiments led science further toward the formulation of atomic theory.

Thanks to Boyle's seminal research with invisible matter, he has been called the "Father of Modern Chemistry." Indeed, at a time when physical experimentation was focused on objects one could observe with the naked eye or a lens, working with air itself was a tricky and unique venture. Boyle's were some of the first successful experiments to expose the inner workings of matter itself, which became the foundation of modern chemistry.

To assist in his various experiments, Boyle hired the English scientist Robert Hooke. Together, they built the air pump that would be the central feature in Boyle's research. The latter used this to demonstrate air vacuums, as well as to prove the necessity of air for the transmission of sound. The pair also worked together to prove how important air was for breathing in animals—including humans. Such research has remained vitally important for a variety of sciences, including medicine, biology, physics, and, of course, chemistry.

Gas pressures, volumes, and uses were by no means Boyle's only scientific interests, however. He was a staunch believer in the transmutation of base metals into gold, and he claimed to have seen such a miracle performed before his own eyes. Unfortunately, back in 1404, King Henry IV of England signed the Act Against Multiplication, which made it illegal to create gold or silver—not that such a thing had actually been achieved, but it was nevertheless a hot topic among alchemists. Boyle was so determined to figure out the mythical method of transmutation that he actually spoke to the English Parliament and convinced it to repeal the law in 1689.[100]

---

[100] Smith, Kiona N. "The Day England Outlawed Alchemy." *Forbes*. January 13, 2018.

Despite his lifelong trials in alchemy, however, Robert Boyle did not succeed in changing lead into gold; he did, however, learn that pure elements and their mixtures with other elements were much more than the sum of their parts. Chemistry, he believed, was a most necessary function of science since it would help scientists break the world down into its smallest and most basic parts. These, he believed, were God's own natural laws.

Chapter 21 – Antonie van Leeuwenhoek

October 24, 1632–August 26, 1723

"I've spent more time than many will believe [making microscopic observations], but I've done them with joy, and I've taken no notice those who have said why take so much trouble and what good is it?"[101]

Just as lenses were being fine-tuned for looking outward to the stars, so, too, were they being developed for the purposes of looking inward at the world. Magnifying glasses and eyeglasses were immensely useful, enabling near-sighted people with the ability to see the world around them much more clearly. The magnifying lens brought vision to the nearly blind so that they could read and write with little difficulty and even journey outside their homes without becoming lost. It was a new era for people who would otherwise have been housebound or unemployable—but, of course, the advent of the lens also had a significant impact on the ongoing Scientific Revolution.

---

[101] Wood, Arron and David Ellyard. *Who Discovered What When.* 2005.

For Antonie van Leeuwenhoek, magnification was something of an obsession. Lenses with very powerful magnification were used in the first microscopes during his lifetime, and the new device enabled him to look into the minute specks of matter that made up larger materials. It was an opportunity to examine the rings and fine grains of wood, to explore the invisible details of insects. Leeuwenhoek used his microscope on anything he could find, indoors or outdoors, and soon, he made a groundbreaking discovery: there were tiny living creatures on the surfaces of many of the objects he put under his lens. In recounting how he had found such creatures living in a drop of water from his own well, Leeuwenhoek described the tiny beings as "little animals or animalcules…This was for me, among all marvels that I have discovered in nature, the most marvelous of all."[102]

Those little animalcules, as Leeuwenhoek called them, were microorganisms. It was now the latter part of the 17th century, and Leeuwenhoek was fascinated by the little animals he found running and swimming on and in nearly everything. For instance, an examination of water revealed clusters of "little eels," and he remarked that there were probably a thousand organisms swimming around in just one drop of water.[103] Leeuwenhoek was delighted to discover an entire world of tiny animals, and he drew figures of the ones he could see most clearly, including what were later determined to be protozoa.

Of some of the tiny organisms, Leeuwenhoek speculated that though he could not determine how they propelled themselves about the world, they may have had sets of tiny paws. In 1774, while describing the summer waters of a lake called Berkelse Mere, the biologist noted that the waters became cloudy in the warm weather. He wrote:

---

[102] Berg, Howard C. *E. Coli in Motion.* 2008.
[103] Ibid.

> At the beginning or middle of summer it becomes whitish, and there are then little green clouds floating in it. [Among the clouds are] green streaks, spirally wound serpent-wise, and orderly arranged. Among these streaks there were besides very many little animalcules…And the motion of most of these animalcules in the water was so swift, and so various upwards, downwards and round about that 'twas wonderful to see: and I judged that some of these little creatures were above a thousand times smaller than the smallest ones I have ever yet seen upon the rind of cheese.[104]

Though Leeuwenhoek had discovered and documented his "animalcules" over the course of several years in the 1670s, it was 1677 when the Dutch lens hobbyist wrote a formal letter citing his groundbreaking discovery of animalcules in water to the Royal Society of London.[105] There, the idea was met with immediate disbelief and criticism; however, a respected Society member, Robert Hooke, took it upon himself to repeat the experiments and see whether Leeuwenhoek's claims could be true. The duplicate experiment worked, and in 1680, Leeuwenhoek was given membership to the Royal Society.[106]

Leeuwenhoek probably only visited London once, in 1668, but he kept up a regular correspondence with the Royal Society after his initiation into the group, sending as many as 190 letters during the course of his lifetime.[107] Though at first he was only a scientist in his free time, the discoverer of microorganisms delved deeper and deeper into natural sciences like botany and anatomy, spending more of his time composing scientific articles. His discoveries were

---

[104] Lane, Nick. "The unseen world: reflections on Leeuwenhoek (1677) 'Concerning little animals.'" *The Royal Society Publishing*. 19 April 2015.

[105] Ibid.

[106] "Antonie van Leeuwenhoek." *BBC History*. Web. 2014.
[107] Ibid.

always relayed to the Royal Society, who published them on his behalf in their journal, *Philosophical Transactions*.

The Dutch biologist didn't know it, but his discoveries would enable future scientists to make huge leaps forward in the understanding of germ theory and vaccine creation. Just as Galileo's discoveries urged humanity forward into the age of the heliocentric universe filled with planets and stars, so, too, did Leeuwenhoek's findings corroborate Boyle's theories that the world was comprised of countless tiny organisms and chemical pieces.

Chapter 22 – Isaac Newton

December 25, 1642–March 31, 1727

"This most beautiful system of the sun, planets and comets, could only proceed from the counsel and dominion of an intelligent and powerful Being."[108]

While at home from Cambridge University's Trinity College during a particularly bad epidemic of the plague, Isaac Newton spent his time studying and pondering the cosmos. Ultimately, he spent eighteen months away from school between 1665 and 1666, and during that time, he began work on some of his most influential theories—including that of gravity. Newton liked to tell people the story of how, as a young student, he had sat in his family garden one day when an apple fell from a tree and struck the ground.[109] It was that event that became the focus of his lifelong study of gravity and the physics of motion.

---

[108] Newton, Isaac. *The Principia: Mathematical Principles of Natural Philosophy.* 1687.

[109] It seems to be a fallacy that the apple struck Newton on the head as there is no documentation to support that particular detail.

After receiving his master's degree in 1668, Newton accepted a fellowship with the university and began teaching there.[110] His first lessons were on optics. During his work with light and lenses, Newton began to create his own telescope. By 1668, he had created a brand-new optical tool that used mirrors instead of the curved lenses used by Galileo and Lippershey. This would be called a reflecting telescope; the type made by Lippershey was a refracting telescope. Lippershey's invention depended on the refraction of light through a series of lenses, while Newton's used a curved mirror to capture the light and then a smaller mirror set before the focal point that reflected the image to the eye of the observer.

Though Newton was interested in the telescope for its astronomical applications, he built his with a mirror in the hopes that it may process light differently, thereby helping him study the properties of the light spectrum. He had become fixated on the way a glass prism would create a rainbow of light from a single beam of normal, white light, and he believed that this had something to do with the tendency of refracting telescopes to distort color. Indeed, his reflecting telescope was free from chromatic aberration, although the final images it produced were upside-down, unlike Galileo's.

Newton presented the Royal Society of London with his second reflecting telescope in 1672.[111] That same year, he became one of the Society's first generation of elite members, where he attended regular meetings with other male scientists to discuss theories and put them to the test. The Royal Society had a royal charter from King Charles II, who had been reinstated to the crown of England, Scotland, and Ireland in 1660 following the execution of his father during the English Civil War.[112] With the king's support, the Royal

---

[110] Hatch, Dr. Robert A. "Sir Isaac Newton (1642-1727)." *Luminarium*. Web. 1998.

[111] Mills, A. A. "Newton's telescope, an examination of the reflecting telescope attributed to Sir Isaac Newton in the possession of the Royal Society." *The Royal Society Publishing*. 1 March 1979.

[112] "Restoration, English History 1660." *Encyclopaedia Britannica*. Web.

Society blossomed into an important center of scientific discussion for all of Europe.

Via his Society connections, Newton was able to build a great reputation for himself as a brilliant scientist. He befriended Robert Boyle and studied his work closely, including Boyle's writing on alchemy, for which Newton had a secret passion. It was at the Royal Society that Newton began discussing his ideas about the physical movements of the Earth and the objects upon it. In 1687, he published the law of gravitation and the three laws of motion in his masterwork, *Philosophiæ Naturalis Principia Mathematica* (or in English, *Mathematical Principles of Natural Philosophy*):

1. Every object persists in its state of rest or in uniform motion until it is compelled to change that state by forces impressed on it.
2. Force is equal to the change in momentum per change in time. For a constant mass, force equals mass times acceleration (F=ma).
3. For every action, there is an equal and opposite reaction.

The law of gravitation claimed that there is a natural force of attraction between any two objects and that must be what keeps the Moon from following the Earth in a circle instead of traveling in a straight line. Newton calculated the attractive force between any two objects with the following equation:[113]

$F = G(m1*m2)/r^2$

So, where F equals the attractive force, or gravity, between two objects, m1 and m2 equal the masses of those objects. The radius of the distance between the objects is demonstrated by r, and G is the gravitational constant. Using this formula, Newton was able to demonstrate that the gravity between two objects increases as the distance between them decreases and that the gravity decreases as the distance between the objects increases.

Philosophiæ Naturalis Principia Mathematica is the book that many historians use to mark the conclusion of the Scientific Revolution; though it certainly solidifies the work of Newton's predecessors in reference to physics, it is difficult to exclude the following discoveries from such a grand era since they so keenly built upon the endeavors of their Renaissance predecessors. The book was well received by the Royal Society, with one major exception: Robert Hooke. Hooke had already published two works on the topic of gravitation, and in a lecture to the Royal Society in 1666, he said the following on the subject:

> I will explain a system of the world very different from any yet received. It is founded on the following positions. 1. That all the heavenly bodies have not only a gravitation of their parts to their own proper centre, but that they also mutually attract each other within their spheres of action. 2. That all bodies having a simple motion, will continue to move in a straight line, unless continually deflected from it by some extraneous force, causing them to describe a circle, an ellipse, or some other curve. 3. That this attraction is so much the greater as the bodies are nearer. As to the proportion in which those forces diminish by an increase of distance, I own I have not discovered it...[114]

Upon reading Newton's own book on the same subject, Hooke immediately attacked his peer via a series of public letters to the Society. The two began a lengthy and very public discourse that would last for decades. Eventually, Newton tired of constantly defending his own scientific merit, and after suffering a nervous breakdown, he retired from research and took a job with the Royal Mint.

---

[113] UCSB ScienceLine. *The Regents of the University of California.* 2017.
[114] Stewart, Dugald. *Elements of the Philosophy of the Human Mind.* 1877.

Chapter 23 – Robert Hooke

July 28, 1635–March 3, 1703

"By the help of microscopes, there is nothing so small as to escape our inquiry; hence there is a new visible world discovered to the understanding."[115]

Robert Hooke was born on the Isle of Wight in 1635, a somewhat fragile boy prone to sickness and allergic reactions. At the age of thirteen, the boy was sent to London to apprentice as a painter. He was not untalented, but Hooke did prove overly sensitive to the noxious smells of the paints. He withdrew from the training and instead enrolled at the Westminster School in London where he learned several languages and how to craft musical instruments.

In 1660, two important things happened in Hooke's life. First, the Royal Society of London was established as a club in which England's most revered scientists and philosophers could convene and conduct research side by side.[116] Secondly, Hooke finalized his work on the law of elasticity. His calculations showed that when stretching solid objects, the total stretch is proportional to the force applied. His studies on stress and stretch were crucial to the

---

[115] Hooke, Robert. "Micrographia: Or, Some Physiological Descriptions of Minute Bodies Made by Magnifying Glasses. With Observations and Inquiries Thereupon." 1667.
[116] Lovell, D.J. *Optical Anecdotes.* 2004.

burgeoning industry of watchmaking, and Hooke personally designed the balance springs for contemporary watches.

A founding member of the Royal Society, Hooke and his colleagues resolved to meet weekly, and after 1672, that meant frequent exchanges with Isaac Newton. Hooke and Newton traded a series of letters after *Physica* was published, in which they wrote veiled insults under the guise of Victorian propriety. Eventually, however, the original animosity faded, and they showed a willingness to try to get along with one another.

> DR. Sir, — At the reading of your letter I was exceedingly pleased and satisfied with your generous freedom, and think you have done what becomes a true philosophical spirit. There is nothing which I desire to avoyde in matters of philosophy more than contention, nor any kind of contention more than one in print; and, therefore, I most gladly embrace your proposal of a private correspondence. What's done before many witnesses is seldom without some further concerns than that for truth; but what passes between friends in private, usually deserves the name of consultation rather than contention; and so I hope it will prove between you and me. Your animadversions will therefore be welcome to me; for though I was formerly tyred of this subject by the frequent interruptions it caused to me, and have not yet, nor I believe ever shall recover so much love for it as to delight in spending time about it; yet to have at once in short the strongest objections that may be made, I would really desire, and know no man better able to furnish me with them than yourself. In this you will oblige me, and if there be any thing else in my papers in which you apprehend I have assumed too… If you please to reserve your sentiments of it for a private letter, I hope you [will find that I] am not so much in love with philosophical productions, but that I can make them yield…But, in the mean time, you defer too much to my ability in searching into this subject. What Descartes did

was a good step. You have added much several ways, and especially in considering the colours of thin plates. If I have seen farther, it is by standing on the shoulders of giants. But I make no question you have divers very considerable experiments beside those you have published, and some, it's very probable, the same with some of those in my late papers. Two at least there are, which I know you have often observed, — the dilatation of the coloured rings by the obliquation of the eye, and the apparition of a black spot at the contact of two convex glasses, and at the top of a water-bubble; and it's probable there may be more, besides others which I have not made, so that I have reason to defer as much or more in this respect to you, as you would to me. But not to insist on this, your letter gives me occasion to enquire regarding an observation you was propounding to me to make here of the transit of a star near the zenith. I came out of London some days sooner than I told you of, it falling out so that I was to meet a friend then at Newmarket, and so missed of your intended directions; yet I called at your lodgings a day [or] two before I came away, but missed of you. If, therefore, you continue…to have it observed, you may, by sending your directions, command…your humble servant,

Is. Newton.[117]

Newton's popularity rose higher and higher in the following decades, as did his standing in the Royal Society. By the time Newton was getting ready to finalize his next book and pursue publishing, his feud with Hooke had cooled considerably—but it was about to be reignited. When Newton's *Opticks: or, A Treatise of the Reflexions, Refractions, Inflexions and Colours of Light* was presented to the Royal Society before publication, it was immediately the source of intense, negative scrutiny.

---

[117] Brewster, David. *Memoirs of the Life, Writings, and Discoveries of Sir Isaac Newton*, vol. 1. 1855.

Hooke was not only one of the original members of the Royal Society, but he was also an expert in modern optics. He took his position in the Royal Society seriously, and he couldn't overlook what he believed were glaring errors in his colleague's work. Hooke's own research had led him to believe that light was composed of waves; therefore, Newton's proposal that it was made of particles was a major source of contention. *Opticks* was highly questioned by Hooke in terms of the author's research methods and scientific conclusions. To make things worse for Newton, Dutch optics scientist and Society member Christiaan Huygens (and a friend to René Descartes) had his own criticism to add—namely, that light moved according to the same principles as water.

Newton apparently reacted quite harshly to the public criticism, arguing heatedly in public and making loud statements in his own defense. Some members of the Royal Society received letters so full of rage from Newton that they became concerned with their colleague's mental state. The fit of anger lasted for months, but Newton never wavered in defending his work. In fact, he adamantly insisted that the discoveries he had made were important to all facets of science.

The animosity between Hooke and Newton grew tenser in the passing months until Newton told some of his colleagues in the Royal Society that he was going to quit his membership. The members did their best to assure Newton that his work was considered to be of the highest quality and that neither his intelligence nor his character was under any true suspicion by the general public or most members of the Society. Ultimately, Newton stayed on with the Society despite taking a respite from research, and his mood eventually improved. When Hooke died in 1703, Newton was made President of the Royal Society, and he published *Opticks* the next year.[118]

---

[118] "Robert Hooke, British Scientist." *Encyclopedia Britannica.* Web.

Chapter 24 – Maria Sibylla Merian

April 2, 1647–January 13, 1717

"Art and nature shall always be wrestling until they eventually conquer one another so that the victory is the same stroke and line: that which is conquered, conquers at the same time."[119]

As the Royal Society of London found its feet and became the center of the scientific community in England, natural philosophers on the continent eagerly pursued their own independent studies. In Frankfurt, and later in Amsterdam, scientific illustrator and naturalist Maria Sibylla Merian pushed ahead in the field of entomology. Born into an artistic family in Frankfurt in 1647, Merian began collecting caterpillars and documenting their life stages at a young age. In 1675, she published her first book of illustrations. In 1679, she published the first volume of a series on caterpillars, and in 1683, she published the second volume. These works included descriptions of the life cycles of the insects, a detailed entomology that had few peers at the time.

Merian's work included detailed drawings of insects in various life stages, which helped to dispel the incorrect scientific theory of her

---

[119] Pomeroy, Sarah B. and Jeyaraney Kathirithamby. *Maria Sibylla Merian.* 2018.

predecessors that insects spontaneously burst into life from piles of rotting material. So-called "spontaneous generation" was a famous theory of the ancient Greek philosopher Aristotle, who noted how the flooded banks of the Nile River in Egypt would suddenly teem with frogs where before there had been none. His observations led him to believe that frogs, therefore, spontaneously generated from the mud. Aristotle's excellent reputation in Renaissance society meant that the majority of his theories were accepted by modern Europeans as the basic foundation of science. Merian, however, observed insects in person, and she was actually one of the first naturalists to do so.

In 1699, Merian and her daughter, Dorothea Maria, embarked on a five-year expedition to Suriname (the expedition was cut short, however, due to an outbreak of malaria). During their time in South America, the two artists settled in the town of Paramaribo, where they had instant access to the jungle landscape. They were able to identify a variety of new insects, as well as add to their collection of samples and create a beautiful collection of drawings for their manuscript. The trip gave Merian the chance to see specimens in a natural habitat altogether different from that of her native Europe, and by working with her daughter, Dorothea Maria received invaluable training in botany and scientific illustration.

In 1705, Merian published *Metamorphosis Insectorum Surinamensium*, which gained fame as both a work of art and of natural scientific documentation. The book was published in Latin and Dutch but was later translated into other languages, and the book is, in fact, still in print today. In the pages of *Metamorphosis*, Merian included sixty engravings that illustrated the insects of Suriname in various stages of development that she had observed. Similar to her caterpillar book, *Metamorphosis* depicted the insects on and around their host plants and included text describing each stage of development. The images were entrancing, with lizards grappling with snakes while protecting their eggs and cockroaches scaling the tall stems of fruit trees. Her book was the first of its kind concerning the natural history of Suriname.

Many natural scientists who came after Merian took on her method of scientific illustration in their work.[120] After Merian died in 1717 following the complications of a stroke two years earlier, many of her paintings were bought by Tsar Peter I of Russia. Dorothea Maria was asked to come to St. Petersburg and work as a scientific illustrator for the Russian Academy of Sciences, and she was the first woman to be employed there.

---

[120] Heard, K. *Maria Merian's Butterflies*. 2016

Chapter 25 – Maria Winckelmann-Kirch

February 25, 1670–December 29, 1720

"Early in the morning (about 2:00 AM) the sky was clear and starry. Some nights before, I had observed a variable star and [Maria] *(as I slept) wanted to find and see it for herself. In so doing, she found a comet in the sky. At which time she woke me, and I found that it was indeed a comet...I was surprised that I had not seen it the night before."*[121]

Maria Margaretha Winckelmann was born in 1670 in Leipzig, in the German state of Lower Saxony that was a part of the Holy Roman Empire.[122] Her father was a Lutheran minister who took it upon himself to tutor her, despite it being out of the ordinary for girls of that period to receive much education outside of reading and writing. When Winckelmann's father died, the girl continued to receive lessons from her uncle.

---

[121] Helly, Dorothy O. and Susan Reverby. "Gendered Domains: Rethinking Public and Private in Women's History: Essays from the Seventh Berkshire Conference on the History of Women." 1992.
[122] Gregerson, Erik. "Maria Kirsch, German Astronomer." *Encyclopedia Britannica.* Web.

The girl showed an early interest in astronomy, so much so that a placement was arranged for her as the apprentice of a local amateur astronomer, Christopher Arnold. Arnold earned his living as a farmer, but he allowed Winckelmann to reside in his home alongside his own family and help him with his hobby. During her time at the Arnold household, the young apprentice met fellow astronomer Gottfried Kirch; the pair married in 1692. This was not what Maria's uncle wanted for her, though, as he had early on decided that his niece should marry a Lutheran minister. Her uncle eventually relented and gave his blessing for the wedding, however, despite Kirch's scientific career and the 30-year age gap between Maria and her older bridegroom.[123]

It was an appropriate match in other ways, not only because the two shared a love of astronomy, but because Gottfried clearly valued the mind and input of women in his field. He had been working with his own three sisters for several years in producing calendars that provided information on moon phases, planetary positions, and the time of the sunrise and the sunset. When Maria joined the Kirch family, she set to work alongside her new sisters-in-law, making astronomical observations and calculations for calendar production.

Because she was a woman, Winckelmann-Kirch was unable to receive instruction at a formal post-secondary educational institution. She had relied first upon her father and her uncle, and later on her husband, to assist in her self-guided learning exploits, and thankfully, most astronomical work during this historical period did not take place within universities. Since Maria could easily join her family at the telescope and learn the appropriate mathematical procedures firsthand, the schooling restrictions of her gender did not actually hold her back as much as it would have in other fields of study.

---

[123] O'Connor, J.J. and E. F. Robertson. "Maria Margarethe Winckelmann Kirch." *School of Mathematics and Statistics, University of St Andrews*. December 2008.

Winckelmann-Kirch worked very closely with her husband at the Berlin Academy of Science, which was founded in 1700.[124] Only Gottfried was permitted to have an official position there as Royal Astronomer, but Maria's unofficial position at the institution nonetheless brought great credit to the academy as well. Maria and Gottfried used the information they gathered from their nightly observations of the sky to calculate data to create calendars, almanacs, sun and moon phases, and sunrise and sunset times, among other information that people found useful. There was a great demand for their in-depth calendars and plenty of work to be done. The couple also began to record weather patterns as early as 1697.[125]

In 1702, Maria became the first woman on record to discover a comet.[126] The comet was also recorded by two other astronomers in Rome, but that surely did not tarnish the experience for Maria. What probably did, however, was the fact that her husband Gottfried published a paper on the new comet without giving her any credit. As the official astronomer of the Berlin Academy, he clearly did not feel it appropriate to acknowledge his wife's discovery, probably because the scientific community was accustomed only to celebrating the achievements of men or perhaps because he felt threatened by any discovery not in his own name. It was not until 1710 that Gottfried corrected the record on the discovery of the 1702 comet, but Maria had already missed out on the honor of having the astral body named for her.

Gottfried died in 1710, and Maria, despite her extensive work and even recognition in astronomy, was not able to continue working at the Berlin Academy despite her many years of work there. Maria

---

[124] "History of the Academy." BERLIN-BRANDENBURG ACADEMY OF SCIENCES AND HUMANITIES. 2010. Web.

[125] Shiebinger, Londa. "Maria Winkelmann at the Berlin Academy: A Turning Point for Women in Science." *Isis*. 1987.

[126] O'Connor, J.J. and E. F. Robertson. "Maria Margarethe Winckelmann Kirch." *School of Mathematics and Statistics, University of St Andrews*. December 2008.

even applied for Gottfried's position of Royal Astronomer but was turned down. She was later offered a position as an astronomer to the tsar of Russia, but she declined as she did not want to force her family to leave Germany.

Winckelmann-Kirch went on to publish her own work on the Aurora Borealis, observations of the Sun, Saturn, and Venus, and to produce calendars for other patrons. She also wrote passionately on the subject of female intelligence, arguing that the "female sex as well as the male possesses talents of the mind and spirit."[127] Her son, Christfried, was eventually named Royal Astronomer at the Berlin Academy of Science. Christfried employed his mother, Maria, and his sister, Christine, as his assistants there. However, Maria was soon forced back out of the academy because of complaints from members about her refusal to blend into the background and keep quiet when visitors came to the school. Christine, evidently less vocal than her mother, was able to stay on.

Maria Winckelmann-Kirch continued to work in private, and she died in 1720 after contracting a fever.

---

[127] McBride, JoEllen. "Maria Kirch was the first woman to discover a comet but her husband took credit for it." *Massive Science.* May 1, 2019.

Chapter 26 – William and Caroline Herschel

November 15, 1738–August 25, 1822 | March 16, 1750–January 9, 1848

"...finding that in [the Moon] there is a provision of light and heat; also in appearance, a soil proper for habitation fully as good as ours, if not perhaps better who can say that it is not extremely probable, nay beyond doubt, that there must be inhabitants on the Moon of some kind or other?"[128]

Caroline and William Herschel were born in Hanover, Germany, then a part of the Holy Roman Empire, in the mid-18th century. Caroline suffered from typhoid as a young child and probably because of that illness only grew to an adult height of just over four feet. William was extensively trained in the musical arts, as his father was a professional musician with the Hanover Military Band. Though the siblings' mother was opposed to sending her daughter to attend school, Caroline learned how to sing later in life when William brought her to England to reside with him. The brother and

---

[128] Letter to Astronomer Royal, Nevil Maskelyne in 1780. Quoted by Patrick Moore, *Patrick Moore on the Moon.* 2006.

sister practiced and performed together on multiple occasions throughout their early adulthood, Caroline singing and William accompanying her on the oboe, violin, harpsichord, or organ.

Though William first found employment as a music teacher in England, he was also an active amateur astronomer. The siblings spent their adulthood working together as mathematicians and astronomers, and Caroline learned these subjects from her brother. Over the course of several decades, William also taught himself many of the more complicated aspects of modern astronomy by way of reading the works of Newton and other contemporary scientists.

William built his own telescopes, improving on Newton's with better glass and bigger and better mirrors. In 1772, perhaps lonely—or perhaps concerned about the sedentary, domestic life forced upon his sister in his absence—William invited Caroline to become his astronomy assistant.[129] She accepted, and in addition to helping William with his many observations and calculations, Caroline helped her brother manage his household.

When William discovered the planet Uranus and its two moons in 1871, he quit teaching music and became a full-time astronomer. Triumphant at his astonishing find, William named the new planet in honor of the British king, George III. Unfortunately for both the astronomer and the monarch, the name "Georgium Sidus" did not stick. Nevertheless, King George III appointed William to be his private astronomer. The latter accepted, and so, the Herschels moved to be nearer to the king and to continue their work in 1782.

William Herschel continued to build and improve on the telescopes used in astronomy, and he experimented and reworked materials in an effort to reflect light better. He even created a better alloy with more copper in it that worked better for his observations. He also experimented and made new mirrors because he found that the

---

[129] "Caroline and William Hershel: Revealing the Invisible." *European Space Agency*. Web. 2019.

bigger the mirror, the better the image. By 1789, Herschel had constructed a twelve-meter (forty-foot) telescope at the Observatory House in Slough, England.[130] It was the biggest astronomical instrument in the world at the time.

William published a paper in 1784 called "On the Construction of the Heavens." In those pages, he put forth a model of how the galaxy and the Milky Way were formed. This was also the beginning of his work cataloging what was known about the universe.

Caroline was officially awarded a salary from the king as her brother's assistant, but she also had her own achievements. She discovered several comets and three nebulae, becoming the first known woman to do such a thing. She published her own work called "Index to Flamsteed's Observations of the Fixed Stars," which was a listing of stars and corrections to earlier information published by various astronomers, both contemporary and historical. This work also acted as an addition to the work of Flamsteed, England's first Astronomer Royal, whose own catalog of stars had been published after his death.

By 1800, William Herschel was studying the heat and light from stars, particularly the Sun. He used filters on his telescope lenses and experimented with splitting light using prisms, and he also studied the characteristics of the separated colors of the prism's refracted light. He was able to document the heat differences between the different types of light, leading to a preliminary understanding of infrared light and infrared radiation.

With the strongest telescopes the contemporary world had ever seen, the Herschels were able to see and collect a vast amount of data. They were able to see and better distinguish clusters of stars that had previously been considered single points of light and more correctly catalog all the previously known and new astronomical bodies.

---

[130] "Today in Science: Uranus discovered by accident." *EarthSky in SPACE*. Web. March 13, 2019.

William died in 1822, and Caroline continued their efforts by reworking William's catalogs and producing an all-encompassing book. She was later awarded a gold medal by the Royal Astronomical Society for this work. In 1888, forty years after Caroline's own death, a newly discovered asteroid was named for her, using her second name: Lucretia.[131] The Herschel Space Observatory was named for William in 2009.[132]

---

[131] Redd, Nola Taylor. "Caroline Herschel Biography." *SPACE.com*. Web. September 4, 2012.

[132] "What is the Herschel Space Observatory?" *NASA Jet Propulsion Laboratory*. Web.

Chapter 27 – Mary Somerville

December 26, 1780–November 29, 1872

"Nothing has afforded me so convincing a proof of the unity of the Deity as these purely mental conceptions of numerical and mathematical science which have been by slow degrees vouchsafed to man, and are still granted in these latter times by the Differential Calculus, now superseded by the Higher Algebra, all of which must have existed in that sublimely omniscient Mind from eternity."[133]

Mary Somerville was a voracious learner right from childhood. She received both encouragement, from those who saw and respected her eager mind, and discouragement, from many who preferred she stick to the activities considered more suitable for girls. Somerville persevered, however, and thanks to her family's support, she was indeed able to cultivate a scientific career for herself.

While her family was not wealthy, it was very well connected. Thanks to her parents' social network, Mary was often given opportunities to learn that may not have otherwise come her way. She, unlike many women of the time, had access to a variety of books, and she learned many subjects all on her own. Mary also received instruction from some supportive educators, who were happy tutoring her in scientific lessons despite her gender. Mary

---

[133] Kathryn A. Neeley and Mary Somerville. *Mary Somerville: Science, Illumination, and the Female Mind.* 2001.

learned all manner of mathematics, astronomy, chemistry, and geography, as well as a contemporary knowledge of electricity. At that time, the Military College at Marlow would print mathematical problems in their journal for the public to try to solve, and Mary eagerly tried her hand at coming up with the complex solutions.

In 1811, Mary received a silver medal for her solution to the journal's Diophantine problem. Diophantine problems are so named for the Greek mathematician Diophantus, who first made a habit of using letters within mathematical equations to represent unknown numbers. Diophantine problems are algebraic, in which the mathematician seeks to find the true value of the unknown numbers. The unknown numbers may only be whole numbers, with no fractions.

Following Mary's successful solution to their problem, the *Mathematical Repository* reprinted their question along with its prize-winning solutions. The following reprint shows that the journal editors gave credit to "a Lady," without stating Mary's name.

XX. PRIZE QUESTION 310, *by Mr.* W. WALLACE.

Find such integer values of x, y, z as shall render the three expressions $x^2 + axy + y^2, x^2 + a'xz + z^2, y^2 + a''yz + z^2$ squares, a, a', a'' being given numbers.

FIRST SOLUTION, *by a* LADY.

Assume $x = an^2 + 2mn$, or $x = an^2 - 2mn$,

Not only was Mary Somerville an exceptional mathematician, but she was also the second female ever to have her work presented to the Royal Society of London, after Caroline Herschel. In 1826, Mary's paper, *The Magnetic Properties of the Violet Rays of the Solar Spectrum*, was read to the members of the Society.[135]

---

[134] Leybourn, Thomas. "New series of the Mathematical Repository." 1806.

[135] Etingoff, K. *Women who Built our Scientific Foundations.* 2014.

Mary, like many of her scientific contemporaries, was incredibly interested in the properties of ultraviolet light. She believed that perhaps it could be connected with magnetic forces, as the Italian scientist Professor Morichini had stated in his own 1813 paper. To test Morichini's claim, Somerville conducted a series of experiments.

First, she focused a ray of light through a crystal prism to separate the white light into its seven components: red, orange, yellow, green, blue, indigo, and violet. Next, she focused the violet part of the rainbow onto a steel needle to impart any inherent magnetic properties into the metal. To test its magnetism, the needle was floated in a dish of water to observe whether it would point to the polar north. Her experiments suggested that the needles used did indeed take on magnetic properties after exposure to violet light.

Women were still not allowed to become members of the Royal Society, however; so, despite interest in Mary's paper, she did not personally address the assembled members. Instead, her husband, Dr. William Somerville, read her work to the Society. The topic of the lecture addressed two ideas that were very much in vogue in the Royal Society and throughout other academic circles in Europe: violet light and magnetism. Because of her reputation with the Royal Society and other intellectual circles, Mary Somerville was the first person to be called a "scientist."[136] The term was coined in 1834 when William Whewell referred to her with this term, mostly because the term "man of science" clearly did not suit a woman. The word was soon added to the dictionary and became commonly used.

Perhaps Somerville's greatest contribution to the scientific world was her ability to explain science in common terms for both the hobbyist and the professional scientist to understand. This was a great boon to the popularization of science to the general public.[137] In 1831, Somerville published a book called *The Mechanism of the*

---

[136] Kirch, S and Amoroso, M. *Being and Becoming Scientists Today.* 2014.
[137] Lightman, B. *Victorian Popularizers of Science.* 2007.

Heavens, which explained the solar system in mathematical terms. She had studied the extensive work of French physicist Pierre-Simon Laplace and attempted to translate his work into a common language. This book became a textbook at the University of Cambridge and was used for decades.

She went on to publish *On the Connection of the Physical Sciences* in 1834. In this book, she combined the progress of several sciences, including physics, geology, chemistry, astronomy, and even botanical science, under the same cover. This book was one of the most popular science books of the 1800s, and it eventually ran to ten editions, translated into both German and Italian. It was probably the most popular science book of its day, dominating classrooms and studies until 1859 when Charles Darwin published his *On the Origin of Species*.

Physical Geography was another book Somerville published in 1848, and it, too, came to be used as a textbook which endured throughout the 19th century. It was the first English book on such a topic, and as such, it serves to whet the appetite of scientific Britain and Europe for more knowledge of Earth's physical landscapes.

In 1869, Mary published *Molecular and Microscopic Science*. This book discussed the burgeoning atomic and molecular theories first posited by scientists like Antonie van Leeuwenhoek and Daniel Sennert, and it also gave extensive information about the sciences of plants and animals. This book was another great success. Shortly before her death in 1871, Mary became the first person to sign the petition for women's suffrage mounted by politician John Stuart Mill; however, it was not successful.

Epilogue

Countless others contributed to the amazing shift in humanity's perception of its place in the world, and unfortunately for many of them, little to no information remains. It's difficult to determine exactly when the Scientific Revolution came to an end, mostly because its existence sparked an ongoing Scientific Age that has transformed the entire world. Where natural philosophers like Paracelsus and Isaac Newton left off, a fresh wave of scientists picked right back up in the 19th and 20th centuries. Still, the research and calculations of the likes of Marie and Pierre Curie, Margaret Burbidge, Albert Einstein, and Felicitas Svejda would have been baseless if not for the hard work already conducted by their predecessors.

The scientists who came after the greats of the Scientific Revolution were—and still are—perfectly aware of their place at the end of a long line of physicians, astronomers, mathematicians, and botanists. Everything, from medical practices and germ theory to spectral astronomy and computer science, has evolved the way they are today due to the countless hours of experimentation and thought—both documented and undocumented—of people like poor Giordano Bruno and the eminent William Harvey.

And yet, it wasn't just the science taking place between the 16th and 19th centuries that changed the world. It was the permission of fathers for their daughters to receive a good education and the hard work of women, with or without permission, to pursue education and work within the burgeoning sciences. Women and people of color were rarely touted for their contributions to the scientific community in those days, but enough of them managed to find some acknowledgment that future generations had more than just wealthy white males to look up to. Furthermore, the fact that women and people of color, like Benjamin Banneker of Maryland, born in 1731, proved their capability among the more privileged intellectuals helped to begin to enlighten the world about the equal abilities of all sexes and all races.[138]

Marie and Pierre Curie worked side by side in their laboratory, trying to discover the source of radioactivity in the chemical elements. They discovered radium, a new element whose intense radioactivity, unfortunately, made both scientists very ill. Marie died in 1895 of radiation poisoning. After her death, the element polonium was discovered among her scientific materials.

Luigi Anguillara's immense contribution to botany is commemorated today by the tomato genus "Angillaria (Liliaceae)." This tomato was named in Anguillara's honor by Robert Brown in 1810.[139]

Daniel Sennert's work on atomic theory was reviewed, studied, and quoted by others for centuries after his death. In 1958, Walter Pagel wrote *Daniel Sennert's Critical Defence of Paracelsus*. In 1961, J. F. Partington discussed Sennert's work in *A History of Chemistry*, and in 1972, Allen G. Debus wrote *Guintherius, Libavius and Sennert: The Chemical Compromise in Early Modern Medicine*. The fact that Daniel Sennert's work has been studied and considered for so long after the fact speaks to the importance of his experiments and the advances made because of them.

---

[138] "Benjamin Banneker Biography." *Biography*. Web. 12 April 2019.

[139] "Anguillara, Luigi - - [The Greatest Book of Botany Ever Written in Italy] ." *ViaLibri*. Web.

In the 20th century, Albert Einstein would overturn Newton's concept of the universe, stating that space, distance, and motion were not absolute but relative and that the universe was more fantastic than Newton had ever conceived. The apple tree at Woolsthorpe Manor, of a special variety called the Flower of Kent, still stands at the site where Isaac Newton pondered the mechanics of gravity in his family garden. The home is now a museum, and Isaac Newton's image has been featured on the now-defunct British £1 paper note.

Even more recently, in 2018, a rare butterfly, *Catasticta sibyllae*, was named after Maria Sibylla Merian.[140] It is clear to see that although these scientists have long since passed, their work will continue to live on to inspire new generations of dreamers and innovators.

---

[140] Laskow, Sarah. "A Rare and Striking Butterfly Is Named for a Pioneering Female Naturalist." *Atlas Obscura*. 6 December 2018.

Check out more books by Captivating History

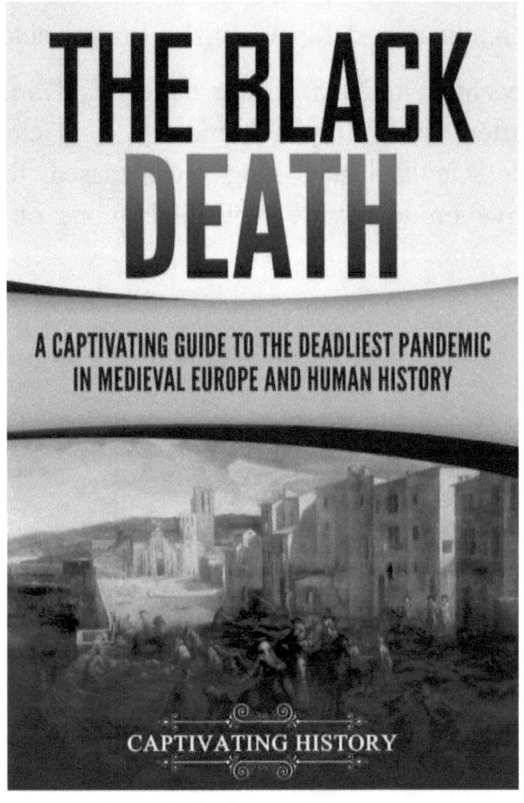

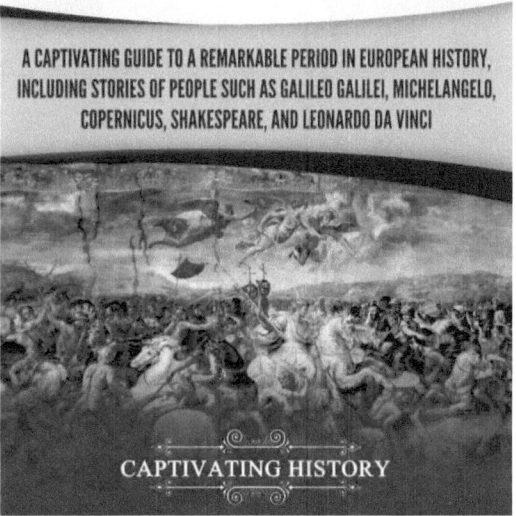

www.ingramcontent.com/pod-product-compliance
Lightning Source LLC
LaVergne TN
LVHW040104080526
838202LV00045B/3770